W9-CGL-669

"This is a well-written book. Also, its mystery stories and activities are entertaining and great for teaching English. *Develop Critical Thinking Skills, Solve a Mystery, Learn Science* is being used with my college students."

Dr. Michael E. Lawson, Professor of English
Suzuka National College of Technology, Japan

"A well-written, effective, and entertaining approach to teaching young people basic scientific problem-solving skills through reading and solving well-crafted mystery stories."

Suzanne F. Smith, University Editor
Clarkson University

"Dr. Barry and Dr. Kanematsu's book is a clever and innovative approach to science education. They not only serve up two mysteries as an intellectual entrée, they offer a guide to applying scientific skills on the side, and top it all off with references to science and learning objectives."

Paul Rader, Science Teacher
Edwards-Knox Central School

Develop **Critical Thinking Skills**
Solve **a Mystery**
Learn **Science**

creative science using two mystery stories

Develop Critical Thinking Skills
Solve a Mystery
Learn Science

with an introduction
by actor **Eric M. Barry**

**Dana M. Barry, Ph.D. &
Hideyuki Kanematsu, Ph.D.**

TATE PUBLISHING *& Enterprises*

TATE PUBLISHING
& Enterprises

Tate Publishing is committed to excellence in the publishing industry. Our staff of highly trained professionals, including editors, graphic designers, and marketing personnel, work together to produce the very finest books available. The company reflects the philosophy established by the founders, based on Psalms 68:11,

"THE LORD GAVE THE WORD AND GREAT WAS THE COMPANY OF THOSE WHO PUBLISHED IT."

If you would like further information, please contact us:
1.888.361.9473 | www.tatepublishing.com
TATE PUBLISHING & Enterprises, LLC | 127 E. Trade Center Terrace
Mustang, Oklahoma 73064 USA

Develop Critical Thinking Skills, Solve a Mystery, Learn Science with Mail Mystery and Mind Games Plus
Copyright © 2007 by Dana M. Barry & Hideyuki Kanematsu. All rights reserved.

Cover design by Sarah Leis
Interior design by Lindsay B. Behrens

Published in the United States of America

ISBN: 978-1-6024707-4-3

07.01.10

Dedication

This book is for our parents:

Daniel and Celia Malloy

Shoji and Michiko Kanematsu

Acknowledgement

We thank our families (especially our parents, Dana's husband, James, her children, James, Brian, Daniel, and Eric, Hideyuki's wife, Reiko, and his children, Hitomi and Hiroyuki), our colleagues, friends, and Tate Publishing for their inspiration and continued support.

Table of Contents

Develop Critical Thinking Skills, Solve a Mystery, Learn Science, which is written in both Japanese and English, is an innovative way to develop and perfect critical thinking skills by reading stories and solving a mystery. It targets upper middle/senior high school students (ages 13–18 years old) and their teachers. The book may also be used by college students and their instructors in teacher preparation courses (for students studying to be elementary and secondary school teachers). This unique book helps students master the steps of a problem-solving model used by scientists and provides them with mental exercises at all levels of Bloom's Taxonomy. It is an interdisciplinary approach for the teaching of science and language (reading). The text includes two short stories ("Mail Mystery" and "Mind Games Plus") and a detailed science education component.

"Mail Mystery" is designed to develop and perfect students' critical thinking and problem-solving skills. It simulates a science research project in that a problem needs to be solved. Students act as detectives to analyze the short story and solve the crime (problem). They master the steps of a problem-solving model used by scientists. Also, they practice mental exercises (thinking like scientists), which help them to identify and creatively solve problems. In addition, "Mail Mystery" includes science vocabulary words and has science lessons built around its contents.

"Mind Games Plus" provides additional mental exercises for students to practice and develop their science process and critical thinking skills. They once again use the problem-solving model included in the book to analyze the story and solve the crime (the problem). This mystery also has laboratory safety rules and exciting science lessons incorporated into its text. One activity simulates the stretching of chemical bonds by using items such as gum, candy, and rubber bands.

The science education component that complements the "Mail Mystery" story includes activities, science vocabulary words, and a problem-solving model, which allows students to act as detectives. They use the model to analyze the story and solve the problem (crime). This model may also be applied to "Mind Games Plus." Students exercise science process and critical thinking skills (used by scientists), as well as master the steps of a problem-solving model.

Develop Critical Thinking Skills, Solve a Mystery, Learn Science is a creative, interdisciplinary teaching approach. It is an excellent resource book for upper middle/senior high school science teachers to enhance science literacy, promote positive science attitudes, and to turn students who enjoy reading onto science. The book includes an introduction (to the mysteries) by Hollywood actor, Eric Barry, who appeared on Dr. Barry's Science Education television show about exotic animals and who performed the science education rap song "Chemicals," featured in Dr. Barry's national award-winning "Chemical Sensation Project" with Dr. Kanematsu of Japan.

Dana M. Barry
Hideyuki Kanematsu

Introduction

People often get jobs, which they expect to be mundane and routine, but quickly realize the opposite to be true. Chaos and mayhem soon erupt. A controlling boss, weird hours, and crazy co-workers are just a few of the possibilities.

That is why I opted to be self-employed. However, that proved not to be financially rewarding, so I tried to break into the film industry as an actor. Within months I was successful, having landed a supporting role as Fidget in the John Waters' film *Cecil B. Demented* (See photo). With this job, I willingly accepted to work fourteen-hour days. Also, I was warned of the tremendous amount of pressure and tediousness that a film demands.

A movie requires about two or three months to film and a commercial requires about one or two days to complete. Therefore, unless an actor signs a multi-year contract for a TV show, every film job is temporary.

Some workers have the same boss for twenty years or more. As an actor, I will have a different boss every year and only for days or months at a time. Everyone needs to have a job. Just make sure you like doing it!

Eric M. Barry

Eric Barry (right) as Fidget with John Waters
on the set for the film *Cecil B. Demented.*

Eric is an actor who lives in California. In addition to his supporting role in the John Waters' film *Cecil B. Demented,* he has appeared as
a guest star on television episodes of *ER, Philly, Boston Public, Judging
Amy, 10–8,* and *Without a Trace.* Also, he has appeared in nation-
ally televised Toyota, Hyundai, and Domino's Pizza commercials. Eric
(Dana Barry's son) is a graduate of Canton Central School (Canton,
New York) and Western Maryland College (now called McDaniel College) in Maryland. He appeared on Dr. Barry's Science Education television show about exotic animals and performed the Science Education
rap song "Chemicals" in Dr. Barry's national award winning "Chemical
Sensation Project" with Dr. Kanematsu of Japan.

Mail Mystery
By Dana M. Barry

Chapter 1

(A fictitious short story that provides interesting and innovative science activities to develop problem-solving and critical thinking skills.)

It was summer vacation and Sue Phillips was home from college. She was hired to be a mail carrier in Rome, New York. Sue was delighted to have a job, but was unaware of the danger that awaited her. (Time Period: 1970s)

Sue Phillips had been home from college one month, and today her summer job as substitute mail carrier started. Sitting at the breakfast table, sipping coffee, and staring at a slice of buttered toast, Sue thought, *Where did the time go?* She had visited some friends, done some shopping, and discussed college life with her folks. That was about it.

"Sue, are you ready to go? You don't want to be late for your first day of work!" yelled Dan Phillips from the bathroom.

Sue's father was a tall, distinguished-looking man who worked for the Air Force Base in Rome, New York. Since Sue was to deliver mail in Rome, they would ride together.

Startled from her train of thought, Sue hesitated and replied, "Yes, I'm ready."

"Good! Let's go!"

They grabbed the lunches that Sue and her mother had packed the night before and headed for the car.

It was about a thirty minute ride to Rome from Clinton, but for Sue, it wasn't long enough. She needed to pull herself together. The reality of the job had just dawned on her. She would be delivering mail in a city that she knew very little about. There would be dogs after her and who knows what else. She had read where just last week a mailman had accidentally been shot delivering mail to a city bar. This job would make her a prime target for danger.

"Sue, are you all right?" inquired Dan. "You haven't said a word for twenty minutes. It is such a nice day. The sun is shining and the birds are singing. You should be happy and enthusiastic on your first day of work!"

"I know, Dad, but I am very nervous about the job. I don't know anyone in the city, nor do I know my way around. Plus, it can be dangerous!"

"In what way?"

"Well, I may meet some strange people, or I may have the misfortune of getting shot like that poor mailman did last week."

"Oh, don't be silly, Sue. That happens one time in a million. You can be healthy today and die of a heart attack tomorrow. Actually, being a mailman is a safe job. For the most part, you are around people, and all the business sections of the city have cops patrolling them. You are worrying about nothing. You will meet lots of people and see the museums and stores. It will be fun."

"I suppose you're right, Dad. I'm acting foolish."

Dan made a right hand turn and pulled in front of a red brick building that had a big blue mailbox out front.

"This is the place. Cheer up and have a nice day. I'll pick you up at 5:00 p.m."

Sue forced a smile and said, "Good-bye, Dad." She watched him drive away until his blue Chevy was out of sight. A sudden chill went through her body. She was now alone and insecure.

2
Summer Job

"Good morning, Miss. Isn't it a beautiful day!" exclaimed a young man briskly climbing the steps to the post office.

He seems sweet and is cute too. Maybe today will be a nice day after all, Sue thought.

After entering the post office, Sue asked to see the person in charge. She was introduced to a small-framed man with blue eyes and grey hair. His name was Mr. Lawrence and he was the postmaster. He told Sue that she was hired for the summer to be a substitute for mailmen on vacation. Mr. Lawrence was a very serious person who talked in a firm and confident voice.

He informed Sue that if she wanted a man's pay, she would be expected to carry the heavy mailbag like the men. He advised Sue to carry Mace on the mail routes.

"Mr. Lawrence, will the Mace really protect me from the dogs?" asked Sue.

"In some cases, the Mace works, but sometimes if you use it, a dog gets angry and is waiting to get even with you the next time he sees you."

"Do many of the mailmen use Mace?" inquired Sue curiously.

"Yes. Some of them also bribe the dogs with dog food," replied Mr. Lawrence.

Mr. Lawrence escorted Sue to the rear of the post office.

"Miss Phillips, I would like you to meet Tom Johnson." Tom was a short, stout man of about forty years of age. Tom offered Sue his hand.

"Pleased to meet you. I am Sue Phillips."

"Tom Johnson will take you on his route today," said Mr. Lawrence.

Sue followed Tom Johnson over to his mail station. The station consisted of a table with a set of shelves on it that contained separate compartments. Tom sorted his mail and grouped it according to streets and numbers. Using rubber bands, he made separate bundles of mail.

"These bundles will be placed in relay boxes along my route," declared Tom.

"Is that how you keep refilling your mailbag when it empties?" asked Sue.

"Yes. That's right," replied Tom.

It was 9:00 a.m. and Sue and Tom were delivering mail in a large brick apartment building that had all of its mailboxes located in the lobby. "This building houses wives and children of servicemen," said Tom in his relaxed, soft-spoken voice.

Farther along the route, Sue noticed a couple of old, abandoned houses that had mailboxes bulging with mail. Tom explained that the deceased owners were still receiving mail.

The morning passed quickly. It was now noon and time to break for lunch. Since it was very hot and humid, Sue and Tom were refreshed when they entered Joe's air-conditioned Bar and Grill. Sue ordered a hamburger and a large coke with ice. Tom ordered the same.

Tom asked, "Do you think you will enjoy being a mail lady?"

Not letting her true feelings of fear and reservation show, Sue casually answered, "It seems to be not only an interesting job, but also one that provides exercise and fresh air."

"I am glad that you see merit in this type of job. Starting tomorrow, I will be on vacation for two weeks and you will be delivering my mail," declared Tom in a serious voice.

"Oh! I see," Sue replied in a disappointed voice.

Isn't he rushing it a bit?

After eating lunch, Tom and Sue finished delivering the mail and returned to the post office. It was 5:00 p.m., and Sue was standing in front of the post office waiting for her father to arrive. It had been a long, hot day and she was tired and sweaty, not to mention her aching feet.

Dan Phillips had a busy day inspecting new homes at Griffis Air Force Base. He was the best inspector on the Base and therefore never ran out of work. He seemed to be rushed all day trying to complete his inspections and arrive at the post office in time to pick up Sue.

This week should be more relaxed, thought Dan. *Five of my children are away at summer camp.*

Sue was the oldest of Dan's six children. She was a pretty girl with brown eyes and long, brown hair. She was a junior at SUNY Potsdam, majoring in chemistry. Sue's high academic average at college qualified her for the summer mail carrier job that started today.

"Screech!" Dan's blue Chevy pulled into the post office parking lot.

"How did your first day of work go?" asked Dan.

"It was okay, but I am exhausted. This job involves a lot of walking. I carried the mailbag for part of the route and found it to be heavier than I anticipated. Thank goodness this is only a summer job. I think I would become hunchback if I were to carry that heavy sack all the time."

"It wouldn't be that bad. You would get used to carrying the sack and barely notice it. I was extremely busy inspecting new homes today and rushed to get over here to pick you up," said Dan.

Dan turned on the car radio. He and Sue remained quiet the rest of the way home. Finally, Dan drove into their driveway. Their home consisted of a double garage and a spacious, brown-shingled ranch house on an acre of land located near Hamilton College in Clinton.

Sue's mother, Angela Phillips, greeted them with a delicious meal of spaghetti and meatballs. Mrs. Phillips was the perfect mother. She stayed home to raise her six children and was always there when they needed her. She was an excellent cook.

Sue described in detail the day's activities to her parents over dinner. She informed them that tomorrow would be her day to solo the route for Tom Johnson, who would be on vacation for two weeks.

Angela said, "Sue, don't worry. The job will go smoothly, and remember, your father is in the city too. You could probably get in touch with him if necessary."

"Mom, I guess I always worry too much. In school I would worry about tests and usually end up with scores of ninety percent or higher. I will take the job one day at a time and try not to worry about it."

Sue helped her mother wash dishes and cleaned up the kitchen. After that, Sue decided to retire for the night since she was thoroughly exhausted and had to rise for work at 6:00 a.m.

4
Strange Discovery

Sue sluggishly entered the post office at 6:50 a.m. and punched the time clock. She would have to punch it again before she left for home. She dreaded the thought of having to solo (work alone) today.

Pull yourself together. You are just working yourself into a tizzy, thought Sue as she organized her mail for the relay boxes. *Things will go smoothly, just like mother said.*

"Good morning, Miss Sue Phillips!" said the soothing voice of the young postal clerk. "My name is James Brown. How is everything going? I see that you have long wool pants on."

"You startled me. I was deep in thought and your voice interrupted it. Oh, my pants—I thought these pants would better protect my legs from dog attacks. As you can see, I am nervous. Today I solo on Tom Johnson's route."

The handsome young clerk with dark eyes and dark hair, said, "Please feel free to ask for my assistance any time. I am always available to help good-looking young women."

"Thank you very much for your offer. I really appreciate it!"

James asked in a serious voice, "Sue, would you like to go to lunch with me today? I could meet you at noon in the Public Library on your route. From there we could go to a cozy little restaurant."

"That would be great, James! See you at noon in the library."

It was a nice, sunny day in July. Flowers were in bloom everywhere and the grass was bright green. Sue's mail delivering seemed to be going well, and she was looking forward to going to lunch with James.

Sue happily thought, *Isn't it great! It is my second day of work, and I already have a date. Soon I'll be in an air-conditioned restaurant with James.*

Sue approached a shabby-looking apartment house surrounded by maple trees and somewhat secluded from other homes. The house was in need of a paint job to say the least.

Some windows were shattered and it looked as though it had survived a recent fire.

Upon entering the house, Sue faced a battered set of stairs that led to mailboxes at the upstairs' landing.

Sue slowly and carefully climbed the creaking stairs. Sounds of shuffling feet and muffled voices penetrated the air.

"Is anyone home? I am the mail-person just delivering mail," mumbled Sue in a weak voice. Sue received no response.

On the landing opposite the mailboxes, an apartment door remained ajar. Sprawled at its entrance lay the body of a woman.

"Ah!" yelled Sue at the top of her lungs. "Miss, are you okay?"

No response.

"Oh my goodness. What should I do? I don't dare touch the body and risk having my fingerprints on it. I must get help."

Sue stood at the doorway peering into the apartment's living room. There must have been a struggle. The phone was dangling on its cord and chairs were overturned. Dirt from a broken planter covered the rug. As Sue was debating whether to enter the room, she heard muffled voices of men, followed by the sound of their shoes descending a back stairway.

"I have to get out of here!" murmured Sue in a frightened voice. "Hopefully those men didn't see me."

She cautiously and quietly descended the front stairs. She gingerly peered out the window of the front door. No one was in sight. Sue made a fast exit.

The library was a few blocks away. Sue decided not to deliver any more mail, but to hurry as quickly as possible to the library and seek the help of James Brown.

Sue breathlessly entered the library with the heavy brown mail sack draped over her shoulder. She felt self-conscious and very noticeable.

Boy, I must be a sight. Everyone is staring at me. Where is James? thought Sue. She looked at her watch. It was only 11:45 a.m. She would have to wait fifteen minutes.

She grabbed a daily paper from the newspaper rack and dropped herself into a vacant chair. Every once in awhile, she peeked around the paper to see if James had arrived.

When Sue was engrossed in an article about Rome Air Force Base, her father's place of employment, she felt a tap on her shoulder. Sue jumped out of her chair with a shriek.

"Excuse me, Miss, I noticed that you were wearing a watch. Could you please tell me what time it is?" asked a nice-looking man of about thirty with black hair and dark blue eyes.

"Oh! You startled me. It's about five minutes before noon."

"My name is Dave. Thank you, Miss . . ."

"Just call me Sue. You are welcome."

Dave stood in front of Sue staring through her with big, icy blue eyes.

If he keeps staring at me, I am going to crack up, thought Sue. To escape from his gaze, she said the first thing that came into her mind. "Nice to meet you Dave, but I have to leave now for an appointment."

Rushing out the library door, Sue collided with James.

"What's the matter, Sue?" asked James. "You look like you have seen a ghost."

Sue hysterically burst into tears.

"Are you sick or did someone attack you? Tell me what happened!"

"I n-n-need to talk to you in a private place," declared Sue in a cracked voice.

"Let's get in my car. It is the white Ford parked directly in front of the library."

After several minutes of silence in James' car, Sue noticed that the red convertible parked in front of them was being driven away by the man named Dave. *Should I tell James about him? No, not now. I must pull myself together and tell James about the body in the dilapidated apartment house.*

"James, you have to help me," squeaked Sue in a weak and frightened voice. "I found a dead body in an old, run-down apartment house about two blocks away. I think the killers were making their escape when I arrived with the mail."

"Did you see them?"

"No! I just heard their muffled voices and their noisy shoes as they quickly descended a back stairway moments after I arrived."

"We must inform the police at once," declared James.

James and Sue entered the police station and described the details of the terrifying incident to Sergeant Miles, a highly respected cop in Rome. He was a rotund man with male pattern baldness. Clearing his throat, he thanked them for the information and said that he would immediately start the investigation. Sergeant Miles bid them good-bye and said he would call them if he needed further assistance.

After leaving the police station, James took Sue for a bite to eat at Joe's Bar and Grill. Sue was too upset to eat, so she just ordered a large soda. James, on the contrary, had a ravenous appetite.

Over lunch, Sue discussed her problems.

"It is 3:00 p.m., and I am emotionally exhausted. My mail needs to be delivered and my father will be soon arriving at the post office."

"Cheer up, Sue," said James in a sincere and reassuring voice. "I will deliver some of your mail. The post office doesn't expect me back today. After asking you to lunch, I requested a few hours of personal leave and got it."

"James, you are a sweetheart and a godsend. I don't know what I would have done without you."

"Sue, you deliver the rest of the mail in your sack. I will pick up the mail in the relay boxes and deliver it for you."

Dropping Sue off at Chestnut Street, James said in a sincere voice, "Finish your route and go home and get a good night's rest. I'll see you tomorrow."

"Are you sure you don't mind delivering my mail? Thanks ever so much. See you tomorrow," said Sue as she waved good-bye to James.

Sue relaxed, took a deep breath, and started delivering mail.

Chestnut Street was picturesque with its colorful flowers, brand new homes, and large weeping willows.

Somehow the brown car with a broken rear window parked on the opposite side of the street doesn't fit, thought Sue.

After having delivered mail to a few houses, Sue was startled by the squeaking brakes of a car that pulled up along side her.

"Hey, honey, how about a ride?" asked a young man in a dark brown shirt. He wore a baseball cap pulled over his forehead to conceal his face. He was in the brown car with the broken window.

"No thanks!" yelled Sue while running to the next house. "I never should have gotten up this morning. Today has been a nightmare. I can't wait to get home."

The brown car slowly drove out of sight.

For the remainder of the block, Sue continued to deliver the mail quickly, staying as far away from the road and sidewalk as possible. The post office had instructed her to use the sidewalks and stay off of people's lawns. Today was different and that rule didn't pertain.

"Whew!" Sue said breathlessly as she slowed her pace to approach a two story house with a screened-in porch and no apparent mailbox. She paused momentarily to catch her breath and to look for the mailbox.

"Hello, Sue," said a voice that came from the porch. "I am Dave from the library."

"Oh, hello!" Sue replied. "Do you have a mailbox?"

"Yes! As a matter of fact, I just bought a new one. Come, I will show you where it is."

Cautiously, Sue followed Dave to the back of the house where the garage and driveway were located. To Sue's surprise, the brown car with the broken window was parked in the driveway. Sue stood frozen in a state of shock.

"Sue, my friend Joe wants to take you for a ride," said Dave in a sarcastic voice as he grabbed her arms. "Joe, get over here with the chloroform," commanded Dave.

Sue struggled to free herself, but it was useless. Dave held her arms very tightly while his friend covered her face with a damp cloth.

Sue collapsed into a state of unconsciousness.

5
Missing

Dan Phillips had another busy day at the Base. There had been many phone calls and a number of housing projects to inspect, but he still managed to arrive at the post office on time to pick up Sue.

Where is she? thought Dan. *I have been sitting in this hot car waiting for nearly fifteen minutes. I better check inside the post office.*

Dan found the door to the post office locked. He saw an open window next to the door.

"Hello! Excuse me, is someone in the post office?" yelled Dan into the window.

"I am sorry, but the post office is closed," echoed a voice from inside the building.

"Please help me. I am here to pick up my daughter, Sue Phillips. Do you know where she is?"

The postmaster immediately opened the door and invited Mr. Phillips in.

"Mr. Phillips, I am Mr. Lawrence, the postmaster, and I am happy to see you. I tried calling you at the Air Base but was unable to reach you. I was unable to reach anyone at your home."

"Oh my goodness! What happened? Is Sue all right?" inquired Dan in an apprehensive voice.

"Keep calm. Don't get yourself worked up." Pointing to a green cushioned chair in front of his desk, Mr. Lawrence said in a coaxing voice, "Please sit down and have some coffee while I tell you what has happened. Our postal clerk, James Brown, met your daughter at noon to take her to lunch. At that time, Sue informed him that she had just found the body of a dead woman in an apartment house. James took

Sue to the police station to report the incident. He then helped her deliver some mail and returned to the post office at 4:00 p.m. to inform me of the situation. Mr. Phillips, your daughter never returned to the post office this afternoon."

Shifting uneasily in his chair, Dan nervously asked, "Is anyone looking for my daughter?"

"Oh, yes, Mr. Phillips!" declared Mr. Lawrence in a very firm voice. "After hearing James Brown's version of Sue's dreadful experience, I immediately sent two mailmen to search for her. When they returned with no clue of her whereabouts, I proceeded to call the police and reported her as missing. At that time I also called the Air Base and your home in vain."

"Mr. Lawrence, I appreciate your concern and I thank you for everything that you have done for my daughter," declared Dan in a melancholy voice. "May I please use your phone?"

"Certainly. Use the phone on my desk."

Angela

Angela Phillips had planned a special meal to celebrate Sue's solo day of delivering mail.

Angela was devoted to her family and enjoyed pleasing them. She spent the afternoon preparing a mouthwatering meal of baked chicken, mashed potatoes, corn on the cob, and homemade rolls. She made a delicious strawberry shortcake for dessert.

The table was set and the food was ready to be served.

Where can Sue and Dan be? thought Angela. She placed the food into the oven to keep it warm. *It isn't like Dan to be late unless—*

"Ring! Ring!"

Angela quickly answered the telephone.

"Oh, Dan, it's you. What's the matter?"

Dan briefly described the day's events to Angela and told her that he would be home shortly.

7

The Investigation

It was late afternoon and Sergeant Miles and his men were investigating the old apartment house where the dead woman's body lay. The house consisted of three apartments, two of which were now empty because the tenants were vacationing.

"What a mess!" bellowed Sergeant Miles as he walked through the wrecked apartment.

Bright red curtains were dangling on unlatched rods, wooden chairs were overturned, books and papers were scattered about, and dirt covered the shaggy white carpet.

A woman's body was sprawled on the living room rug near the entrance door of the apartment. She was wearing a mint green dress with matching heels. Her convulsed face resembled one in intense pain.

"Her name is Leslie Jones. She is thirty years old and is a secretary for the city law firm Briggs and Grows. Forensic scientists even came to collect fibers and hairs for testing," reported Policeman Smitty, a dedicated and energetic cop.

"Good work, Smitty! Did you also find out the time of death?" inquired Sergeant Miles.

"Yes sir! The medical examiner says that Miss Jones had been strangled at approximately 11:00 this morning."

"That is in agreement with a statement made by Sue Phillips, the missing mail carrier who reported the murder. Her disappearance must be connected with this crime. We must find her at once!" commanded Sergeant Miles.

Opening her eyes, Sue found herself fully dressed in a strange bed, surrounded by darkness and the faint smell of smoke.

Rising to a sitting position, she looked around the room, hoping her eyes would adjust and be able to focus in the darkness.

"What has happened? Where am I?"

Reflecting a moment, Sue recalled the last thing she could remember—her arms being tightly squeezed and a damp cloth being dropped over her face. She felt like screaming but refrained.

Thank goodness there is a full moon tonight. I can just barely make out the layout of this room. For the moment it appears empty, thought Sue.

After quietly climbing out of bed, Sue cautiously moved hand over hand along the wall, hoping to find a door or open window. To her surprise, the end of the room contained the main door to the house.

Clutching the doorknob securely, Sue slowly turned it and pulled it open a crack.

Cautiously peering out, she noticed that someone was sitting on the porch smoking. The person didn't seem to notice her. Carefully and noiselessly, she closed the door.

"Whew! That was close," murmured Sue.

"Going somewhere, Sue?" yelled Dave as he tightly grabbed her shoulders from behind and shook her.

"I, uh, uh . . ."

"Dave, what are we going to do with her?" inquired Joe as he entered the house after hearing the noise.

"I'm not exactly sure. She was at the scene of the murder. I saw her approach the old apartment house seconds after the crime was committed," declared Dave. He shoved Sue into the wall and released his grip.

"I know," said Joe. "We barely got away!"

"But I didn't see anything happen!" Sue shrieked in a terrified voice. "Please don't hurt me."

Dave said in a firm voice, "In our business, we can't take chances. You could have seen us or our car and reported it to the police. I followed you to the library and asked you for the time. You appeared to be scared and anxious to get away from me."

"I wasn't afraid of you. I had never seen you before. I was upset and frightened because I had discovered a dead body," whimpered Sue in a cracked voice.

"As I told you before, in our business, we can't take chances. We were determined to capture and silence you. After you got away from me in the library, I sent Joe after you in his car."

Crying and speaking in a semi-audible, pleading voice, Sue said, "Please let me go! I won't tell anybody anything. I only told the police that I found a woman's body in an old apartment house."

"It's too late now. You can easily identify us and our cars," declared Joe.

"It's a pity that we have to silence you. You are pretty, especially in the moonlight," said Dave in a sweet voice as he stroked Sue's hair and gently kissed her cheek. "You have nice long brown hair and lovely brown eyes."

Sue hopelessly dropped to the floor and burst into hysterical crying.

"Dan, I can't sleep!" said Angela in a sad voice as she looked at her illuminated alarm clock. It was 4:00 a.m., and Angela had seen each hour since midnight. Soon it would be time to get up.

"I am worried about Sue."

"I know how you feel, dear," mumbled Dan. "I can't sleep either. The police are doing everything they can. That Sergeant Miles is very intelligent. Last year he almost single-handedly caught the professional robbers in Rome. I have confidence in him."

"Do you think our Sue will be found?" queried Angela in a hopeful voice.

"I hope so," said Dan in a serious voice. "We must pray for her."

10
Sergeant Miles

It was the day after the murder and Sergeant Miles was questioning solicitors Johnathan Briggs and Nathan Grows.

"How long has Leslie Jones been employed here?" inquired Sergeant Miles.

"She has been here serving as our secretary just under three years," replied Nathan Grows, looking over horn-rimmed glasses.

"Did Miss Jones report for work yesterday?" asked Sergeant Miles as he rubbed his fingers over his double chin.

"Yes, she did," declared the solicitors in unison.

"Did either of you notice anything unusual in her manner?"

"She appeared nervous and in a hurry. I just thought she was rushing to complete her work before she left for her morning appointment," surmised Johnathan Briggs as he puffed on a cigar.

"Do you know where she went for her appointment?" inquired the sergeant.

"No! We don't like to get involved in our employees' personal business," replied Nathan.

"Do you know if Miss Jones had any enemies? Can you think of anyone who wanted her dead?"

"No! We didn't really know her well. She came to work, did her job, and then went home. She was quiet and kept to herself," replied Nathan.

"Did she have any friends?"

"Leslie did have a boyfriend whom she brought to our spring office party. His name was Joe something. I only saw him once and can't remember his last name," declared Johnathan.

"I don't recall his last name either," echoed Nathan.

"Gentlemen, thank you very much for your assistance. I will call you if I have further questions," said Sergeant Miles as he hastily left the office.

Mr. Lawrence, the postmaster, was dragging at work this morning. He was upset and had spent much of the previous night worrying about Sue Phillips. He felt guilty about her disappearance.

"If only I hadn't made her solo yesterday then maybe . . ."

"Hey, Mr. Lawrence, who is going to deliver Sue's mail?" asked mailmen Jackson and Peterson.

"What? Oh, yes—Sue's mail. I was lost in thought. Could you guys deliver her mail after you complete your own routes? I will pay you for the overtime."

"Okay, Boss!"

"Good!" replied Mr. Lawrence. "Also inquire about Sue along the route. Maybe we can get some clues as to her whereabouts."

Sergeant Miles entered the post office.

"Excuse me, Mr. Lawrence. May I have a few moments of your time?" asked Sergeant Miles.

"Certainly. What can I do for you?" replied Mr. Lawrence in an arduous voice.

"I just want to ask a few questions. Who was the last person at the post office to see Sue yesterday?"

"I believe it was James Brown, our clerk. He took her to lunch and helped her deliver mail in the afternoon."

"May I please speak to him?"

Mr. Lawrence yelled over to the clerk's desk, "James, come on over here! Sergeant Miles wants to talk to you!"

Rushing toward Sergeant Miles, James said in a hopeful voice, "Have you found Sue yet?"

"No, I haven't. Apparently, you were the last person to have seen Sue before she disappeared. Please tell me when and where you last saw her."

"Let's see. I dropped her off at Chestnut Street, near the stop sign, shortly after 3:00 p.m. I told her to deliver the mail in her mail sack and that I would deliver the rest for her. She thanked me and I drove off."

"Did you notice anything unusual when you dropped her off?"

"No, although I didn't really pay much attention to my surroundings," replied James.

"Thank you for your time, James. I will contact you if I have further questions. Good day!"

Sergeant Miles pensively walked out of the post office. Solving this crime will be like solving a jigsaw puzzle. I have a few pieces, or clues, but I need more and will have to fit each into its proper place. *What is the motive for the crime? Who wanted Leslie Jones dead, and why? Why did Sue Phillips disappear? Was Sue a witness to the crime?*

It was daytime and Sue was seated at the kitchen table with Dave and Joe. Peering out the large window in front of her, Sue could see the dirt road that led to this secluded house in the woods.

"Sue, you will need strength today. Do you want more coffee and toast before I leave to do some errands?" asked Joe in an anxious voice.

"No, thank you," Sue mumbled weakly. She had been so hungry that she wolfed down three slices of toast and a cup of coffee in under ten minutes.

"Dave, I am leaving now and will be back in a few hours. You take care of Sue as planned!" bellowed Joe before slamming the door behind him.

"Alone at last," said Dave as he stood beside Sue's chair. "Now you and I can go for a walk in the woods."

Dave pulled Sue to a standing position and dragged her out the front door.

"Where am I? What are you going to do?" shrieked Sue as she tried to free herself from Dave's grip.

"You are in the country. I intend to have some fun with you before I kill you," replied Dave in a threatening voice. He gently touched Sue's shoulder. Then he shoved her to the ground.

"Run and scream. No one will hear you!" roared Dave as he retreated to get something from his car.

Sue got to her feet and started to run along the dirt road. Her heart beat faster than ever.

Dave stood laughing as he put on a pair of black leather gloves. He was now ready to stalk his prey.

Glancing behind her, Sue noticed that Dave was advancing quickly. *I can't outrun him, but maybe I can lose him in the woods. God, please help me*, thought Sue.

Sue swerved to the right and entered the woods. Completely disoriented, she quickly scanned the area for a large tree and hid behind it.

Dave slowly entered the woods. He paused and yelled, "Ready or not, Dave is coming to get you!"

Upon hearing Dave's approaching footsteps, Sue breathlessly darted from behind the tree.

She ran farther into the woods, dodging tree stumps, rocks, and holes.

"There you are!" cried Dave as he increased his pace to a run.

Sue anticipated his overtaking her at any moment. The situation was hopeless.

Lunging forward to grab Sue by the neck, Dave caught his foot in a woodchuck hole.

Screaming in pain, he fell to the ground.

Sue stood frozen in fear. She watched Dave massage his ankle. He was yelling and tears were pouring down his face.

"Don't just stand there, Sue. Get over here and help me!" commanded Dave as he sat on the ground cradling his foot.

This is my chance to get away, thought Sue. She took advantage of the situation. Sue cautiously moved toward the dirt road, hoping it would eventually lead to safety.

The dirt road seemed to go on forever but it finally intersected with a regular road.

Exhausted and very thirsty, Sue barely trudged along in hopes of flagging down a car. Two passed but neither stopped.

I feel so dizzy that I can't go on any farther, thought Sue. She fell to her knees and vomited.

Glancing toward the road, Sue noticed a white car pull up next to her and stop. Somehow it looked familiar.

"Miss, are you all right?" asked the concerned driver.

When the young man kneeled next to her, Sue recognized his face. He was James Brown from the post office.

"James, please help me," uttered Sue as she collapsed into his arms.

13
The Diary

It was 4:00 p.m. and Sergeant Miles was seated at his office desk deep in thought.

Smitty rushed into the Sergeant's office yelling in an excited voice.

"Sarge! Here is a diary that we found in Leslie Jones' apartment. It contains names and other valuable information."

"That's great, Smitty! It seems like every time I hit a snag in a case, you come to the rescue."

Smitty smiled contentedly and made himself comfortable in a cushioned chair next to Miles' desk. He glanced over a recent issue of *Popular Mechanics* while Miles perused the diary.

Flipping the pages of the diary, Sergeant Miles found the entry for May 15, 1970.

May 15, 1970- Joe Larson escorted me to my annual office party. It was held at the Big Apple in Rome. We had drinks and a delicious ham dinner. We left early because Joe had an appointment with some friends.

Skipping ahead in the diary, Miles' eyes focused on an entry for June 20, 1970.

June 20, 1970- I spent the day at Joe's cozy home in the woods. We were alone, and I confided to him what I had suspected for some time. I told him that I knew he and his buddies were running a large drug ring in Rome. Joe became very upset upon hearing this.

Sergeant Miles read the last entry in Leslie's diary.

July 8, 1970- After work, I stayed home and watched television. Joe called and said that it was very important that he meet me at my apartment tomorrow morning.

"Smitty, this diary contains the missing pieces to my jigsaw puzzle," said Sergeant Miles in a pensive but enthusiastic voice.

"What do you mean, Sarge?" asked Smitty curiously.

"I have been comparing this case to a jigsaw puzzle. It is hard to complete a puzzle when pieces are missing. The muffled voices that Sue heard while delivering mail to the old apartment house must have belonged to Joe and his buddies. Enough of that. Time is running out. You and I need to pay Mr. Larson a visit. Smitty, get the directory on the shelf under the clock and look up Joe Larson's address. Apparently, he was Leslie's boyfriend, and he may be involved in drugs."

"I found it. Let's go see him right now, Boss!"

Both cops immediately left the office.

14

Narrow Escape

James placed an ice pack over Sue's forehead as she lay silently on a multicolored couch in front of him.

"Sue, can you hear me?" inquired James as he leaned over her.

Feeling chilled, Sue opened her eyes to find James' face only inches away.

"What happened? Where am I?" murmured Sue as she reached for his shoulders.

James helped Sue into a sitting position and offered her a large glass of water. Then he yelled across the room, "Sue is awake now!"

"Hope you are feeling energetic, Sue. You got away from me in the woods, but you won't get away this time!" boasted Dave as he limped toward her with outstretched hands that were covered with black leather gloves.

"James, how could you do this to me?" shrieked Sue as she sprang from the couch in an attempt to escape.

"Sue, I am truly sorry, but you have to be silenced. We are running a large drug ring in Rome and don't want to be caught by the cops," declared James.

Hysterically stumbling across the room, Sue caught her foot on a chair leg and fell to the floor. James and Joe immediately dragged her to a standing position. They held her arms tightly behind her back as she screamed wildly.

Dave hurled himself forward and fastened his fingers around Sue's throat.

"Sarge, there is a lot of commotion coming from Joe's house," commented Smitty as the cops approached the entryway.

"Yes, and I don't like it. Get your gun ready. We are going in," whispered Sergeant Miles in an assertive voice.

Sergeant Miles kicked the door open.

"Freeze with your hands up!" he commanded. "Smitty, handcuff them!"

"How did you find out about us?" asked Joe in a defeated voice.

"You were very clever, but you overlooked one major item—Leslie's diary. It contained the missing pieces to my jigsaw puzzle: names, places, and motives!" bellowed Sergeant Miles.

"James and I are innocent. Dave strangled Leslie and Sue!" yelled Joe excitedly.

"You two are accomplices to murder, not to mention your drug dealings. That makes all of you guilty. All of your names are mentioned in Leslie's diary. Joe, you set up Leslie's appointment with death. James, you made sure that Sue would fall into a similar trap. You purposely took personal leave the day of the murder. When you met Sue for lunch and heard that she had discovered a body, you knew she had to be silenced. To draw suspicion away from yourself, you brought Miss Phillips to my office to report the incident. Shortly thereafter, you made plans with Dave and Joe."

"Sarge, congratulations on solving the case. I finally met someone more ingenious than myself," commented Dave as he and his buddies were escorted to the police car.

15
Party

"Sue is home from the hospital and seems to be in good spirits, and those awful men are in prison where they belong. Dan, let's have a welcome home party for Sue," suggested Angela.

"It sounds like a great idea. Let's invite our friends and some postal workers."

"Dear, let's also invite the cops, Smitty and Sergeant Miles. We owe Sue's life to them," declared Angela.

"Yes. That is true," answered Dan.

Angela spent the next few days preparing for the party. She would have barbecued chicken, hot dogs, assorted salads, drinks, and of course her famous homemade apple pie for dessert.

Mind Games Plus
By Dana M. Barry

Chapter 2

(This fictitious story provides activities to develop problem solving and critical thinking skills. Also have the students use the problem-solving model to write a "Report of Investigation" for this mystery. Refer to Chapters 3 and 4.)

A newly hired science teacher encounters many strange people and events and then mysteriously disappears. (Time Period: 1990s)

After completing college, Ann Philips moved to Northern New York to be near her boyfriend, a chemistry teacher in an area school. She liked the North Country with its picturesque landscapes and waterways but felt the job opportunities were very limited for her. Ann was living on money that she had earned during the summer while working as a laboratory assistant at a community college. It was now August and her cash flow was low. She desperately needed a job. She would take anything just to be able to stay near her boyfriend, Bill Jackson.

Ann loved Bill. He was everything a woman could want: charming, handsome, intelligent, caring, and entertaining. He was also an excellent teacher. Ann met Bill in a chemistry lab at college. He was her lab instructor freshman year and spent many hours tutoring her. Eventually, those meetings turned into socializing and dating. Thanks to Bill, Ann received an A in the chemistry lab course and eventually graduated with degrees in chemistry and science education.

"Come in," Ann yelled in reply to a loud knock at her front door.

"Hi, honey. Are you ready to go out to dinner?" inquired Bill. It was 5:00 on Friday evening. Most Fridays Ann and Bill went to Jack's Eatery for the fish fry special.

"Oh my, is it 5:00 already? I guess I got lost in thought and the hours just passed."

Bill, who had been standing in the entranceway, walked into the kitchen and stood in front of Ann. He was a tall, medium-build young man with thick brown hair and dark eyes.

"What have you been thinking about?" he asked in a concerned voice.

Ann was seated at the kitchen table. She turned her head of shoulder-length brown hair and fixed her eyes on Bill. "Oh, I was reminiscing about the good times and when we first met in the chemistry lab. I was also preparing a plan of attack for a job interview that I have on Monday."

"This coming Monday? What type of job is it? Remember, if you want the job, you need to sell yourself. Maybe you can do something unique to get their attention and set yourself apart from the other applicants."

"Yes. Maybe I could stand on my head. The interview is for a science teaching position, so I am somewhat excited about it. I received the interview offer in today's mail. Upon opening it, I immediately phoned the school to set up the appointment."

"That's great. Come on. Let's go plan for your interview over dinner."

Ann smiled and said, "Okay."

2
Interview

Ann was sitting in the high school office with summer school students, whom she assumed to be written up by teachers for discipline problems. They were speaking unkindly to each other and squirming in their seats.

A pleasant secretary with white hair, glasses, and a genuine smile said, "Miss Philips, the principal will be with you in a moment."

"Okay," Ann said.

"Good afternoon, Miss Philips. I'm Mike Jones, the high school principal."

"Nice to meet you," said Ann as she stood up and extended her hand to greet him.

"Please follow me," he gestured. "The teachers are anxious to meet you." He towered over Ann as he led her down a long, dark corridor to a classroom across from the gym. As Ann entered, she noticed three people quietly seated at a round wooden table.

Mr. Jones had thick, curly blond hair and large blue eyes. He displayed a genuine smile that seemed to be glued to his face. In a polite and somewhat excited voice, he introduced Ann to the group. John Smith, the physics teacher, was a tall, muscular man with dark hair and a dark complexion. Linda Ames, the biology teacher, was a short, rotund woman with glasses and a friendly face. The third person at the table was Dr. Joe Law, the school superintendent. He was a short man with brown hair and glasses. Dr. Law appeared neat as a pin and his clothes were pressed to perfection.

"Miss Philips, please take a seat. We have checked your references and you have been highly recommended," said Superintendent Law in a mild-mannered, soft-spoken voice.

Ann thought a moment, *I guess my college professors wrote outstanding letters on my behalf.*

"So you want to teach chemistry?"

"Yes. That is my main area of interest." Deciding to embellish her answer, she continued enthusiastically, "I thoroughly enjoy teaching and being with students. I would love to do extracurricular activities too."

"Good! We are happy to hear that. We want a dedicated teacher who will give our students an excellent science education so that they can compete with students from larger schools. In this small town in the country, the school is the center of attraction for the community."

"Ann, do you have any questions?" piped in Principal Jones.

"Yes. Please tell me exactly what this job involves."

"This is a very easy job, so you should have time to do extras like coaching and organizing clubs."

"Really? What courses would I be teaching and how many sections of each?"

Principal Jones quickly answered, "I believe that you would be teaching eighth grade science and high school chemistry, but we haven't determined the number of sections of each yet."

"I see," said Ann. She noticed that the biology and physics teacher continued to sit quietly through the interview saying absolutely nothing.

The principal fixed his eyes on Ann and spoke again in a concerned voice, "Is that item on the table in front of you melting? It looks like a huge block of ice."

Ann hoped that someone would notice her five pound object, partially covered with a dishtowel. It was her attention grabber for the interview and a way to show her creativeness.

"Don't worry. It isn't melting. This is a piece of glass that resembles ice." Ann held the glass, which was shaped like a miniature glacier, in front of the group to examine. "I brought this glass to show you how I would capture the students' attention to teach them about the phases of matter; solids, liquids, and gases. One could say that the piece of glass looks like a solid, but is really a super cooled liquid."

"That's very interesting. You certainly got my attention," he exclaimed.

The group smiled in unison.

"Any other questions or comments?" inquired Superintendent Law.

The room remained silent. The quiet teachers reminded Ann of puppets.

He continued, "Miss Philips, we want to be certain that our teachers know the subjects they teach. Therefore, as part of the interview, we require the science candidates to take the regents."

Ann rose to attention.

"But I don't want to—"

Before she had a chance to complete what she started to say, the principal put his hand on her shoulder and coaxed her down the corridor to a small classroom.

"You will be comfortable and undisturbed here. When you complete the exam, please return to my office."

He closed the door and walked away.

Sitting alone, Ann deliberated over the options of answering the test questions or walking out and returning home. Her eyes searched the room for an answer. It was a small room with a low ceiling and a freshly mopped green floor. Two of the walls were lined with books and the one opposite her contained a large picture window. Looking through it, Ann saw a three-dimensional movie with cars driving by, beautiful maple trees, and green grass. She longed to be part of this movie. To say the least, Ann was unhappy and needed to make a decision fast.

Ann answered twenty-five of the sixty regents' questions. Then she quickly headed toward the office. She met the physics teacher, John Smith, standing a few feet in front of the door.

Ann sadly said, "I only answered a few of the questions. I'm going home. I don't really need this job."

"Ah, don't worry about it. Everything will be fine." In a reassuring voice he said, "I'm correcting the test anyway. Come on in."

Ann shook her head in the affirmative and followed John into the office.

Principal Mike Jones greeted them with a gigantic smile. Superintendent Law and the biology teacher, Linda Ames, were standing next to him.

Mike excitedly said, "We have all decided to offer you the job. Do you accept it?"

Being shocked and pleasantly surprised by this unexpected offer, Ann blurted aloud "Yes!"

"That's great! Congratulations," exclaimed the robotic group in unison.

"Oh, by the way, we should have your class schedule ready on the first day of school. Relax and enjoy the remaining days of vacation before school starts," said Dr. Law in his soft-spoken voice.

"Thank you. I will. See you all very soon," Ann replied happily as she left the room.

3
Canoe Trip

While driving home, Ann was on an all-time high. She couldn't wait to tell Bill the exciting news. He would never believe that she was offered the job on the spot. She couldn't believe it either. Ann had heard of and even experienced love at first sight, but that was about it. Her memory of that event was as vivid as the day it happened. It was a cold and snowy lunch period during Ann's sophomore year in high school. The students danced to rock and roll music in the gym for their lunch-hour entertainment. Ann, who loved to dance, was walking around and weaving between dancing couples in search of a partner.

"You are beautiful. Would you like to dance?" asked a new student, whom Ann had never seen before. He was cute with brown wavy hair and a charming voice. "I just noticed you from across the gym and my heart sank."

Ann, who was startled by the handsome stranger standing next to her, couldn't believe her ears. She immediately replied, "I'd love to!"

They joyfully danced together all afternoon. It was a wonderful experience that she would never forget.

_____

Ann's mind came back to reality when she drove into her driveway. Of course, she was still very excited about the new job. She quickly entered the house and dialed Bill's phone number.

She wanted to burst out her surprise but decided to keep it a secret for at least a few hours.

"Hello, honey, I am ready to go canoeing."

"Okay, dear. How did your interview go? You sound almost breathless."

"I am in good spirits because the interview went well."

"That's good. You can tell me all about it later. I will pick you up in thirty minutes."

Bill arrived in thirty minutes as stated. He was always on time or early, but never late. His red fiberglass canoe was strapped to the top of a white Reliant. Bill got out of the car and stood with his eyes fixed on Ann. She was dressed for swimming. She looked beautiful in her two-piece, gold sequined bathing suit, which made her look slim. Her long brown hair swayed in the breeze.

"Do you like my new swimsuit?"

"Yes. It looks great on you. Are you going canoeing like that?"

"Not exactly. I just wanted you to see my new suit," Ann said as she quickly slipped a long shirt over her bathing suit. She also put on a white hat to protect her from the sun.

"Hop in the car and let's go."

It was the perfect day for canoeing. The sun was shining. The water was clear, and images of trees and flowers reflected beautifully in it. They were alone on the water. Ann sat in the front casually paddling and periodically running her fingers through the warm water. Bill, on the other hand, steered the boat to dodge dead trees and areas of shallow water in the narrow river passages.

Upon entering a large area of open water, they both stopped paddling and sat in silence, waiting for glimpses of wildlife. A wild blue heron flew over head and they saw a beaver laboriously dragging logs to its home. Ann was completely relaxed and imagined that she was in another world. It was time to share her secret with Bill.

"Bill, guess what? I was offered the job today and took it."

"You're kidding!"

"No. I'm serious. The melting ice trick really caught their attention. That was a good idea," said Ann with a sparkle in her brown eyes.

"What else happened?"

"Actually, the whole event was very strange. During the interview, the teachers sat silently and the principal and superintendent did all of the talking. I was escorted to a small classroom and asked to take the chemistry regents. As you can guess, I was insulted and upset by that request. I debated whether to take the test or to walk out and go home."

"I assume that you took the exam."

"To tell you the truth, I answered less than half of the questions. Then I went to the main office to tell the principal that I was no longer interested in the job. To make a long story short, I was basically offered the job at that time. I was so excited that I accepted it on the spot."

"Ann, I hope you made the right decision," said Bill as he started paddling again. "What courses will you be teaching?"

"That's a good question. I won't know the answer until the first day of school. However, I was assured that it wouldn't be a difficult job and that there would be time for me to run the science club."

"The whole thing sounds pretty weird to me. Hopefully it works out for you. Congratulations!"

Now the sun was setting. They had talked and paddled for hours. The sky was turned into a stunning display of colors. The varying shades of pink, red, and violet combinations were breathtaking.

Ann arrived home at 10:00 p.m. . It had been a long, exciting day for her. Her arms and back ached from hours of paddling and sitting. Thoroughly exhausted, she quickly showered and crawled into bed.

4
First Day of School

It was the first day of school. Ann arrived extra early to find out her class schedule. As she entered the building, Principal Jones unexpectedly greeted her.

"Good morning, Miss Philips. I have been waiting for you," he said in a firm voice. He had a serious expression on his face too. "Here is your class schedule."

"Good morning," replied Ann as she quickly glanced over the list of courses. She was so shocked that her mouth dropped open.

She said in a forced voice, "I didn't agree to teach all of these courses. You have me scheduled for Earth Science, General Science, Physical Science, Chemistry, and their labs. You even expect me to run the Science Club."

Turning his lips into a smile, Mr. Jones said in a reassuring voice, "Don't worry. It's not that bad. Besides, John Smith, the physics teacher will help you. He is your mentor."

Ann lowered her head and walked away in silence. It was all she could do to fight off the tears swelling in her eyes.

She entered her empty chemistry classroom on the second floor. It was large and impressive. The room was rectangular with a chalkboard and demonstration table in the front. Student desks and chairs were in the center of the room, and the lab tables were in the back. The left wall of the room contained a continuous row of windows, exposing the beautiful land and trees that lay beyond. On the right wall hung an assortment of science charts. Ann closely examined the large Periodic Table of the Elements. To ease her mind, she thought about interesting activities for her students to do in the future.

Periodic Table Activity

She would start out by briefly describing the layout of the Periodic Table. She would tell the students that the vertical columns are called groups, or families, and the horizontal rows are known as periods. She would include the following information in her discussion.

Most of the elements on the table are metals. Their atoms lose electrons to form positively charged ions. Consider the sodium (Na) atom found in table salt. It loses an electron to form Na^+. This positive sodium ion combines with the negative chloride ion (Cl^-), formed when an atom of chlorine gains an electron that has a negative charge. The opposite charges attract to form table salt (NaCl, which is really Na^+Cl^-).

Metals are usually solids at room temperature, good conductors of heat and electricity, and have a metallic luster. The strongest metals are on the left side of the table.

The nonmetals are mainly found on the right side of the table. Their atoms gain electrons to form negative ions like the chloride ion. They may exist as gases or dull solids and are poor conductors of heat and electricity.

1. Students Design a Periodic Table

Each student is provided with fifteen different items such as paper, rulers, pens, coins, and magnets. They analyze these items and design a periodic table for them. The table may be organized according to shape, size, color, and magnetic properties, or by some other creative scheme. (Hint:: Consider the layout of a grocery store. The dairy products are together, while the meat is located in another section.) Have the students discuss and display their tables in class.

2. Students Research Their Favorite Elements

Each student selects a favorite element and prepares a written report about it. Then they orally share the information with the class.

Startled by a sudden noise at her open door, Ann looked up in surprise.

"Hi! Do you remember me? I'm John Smith, the physics teacher," he said with a big smile as he marched into the room. "We both have the first period of the day free. I am down the hall from you. Just give a yell whenever you need something. Linda Ames, the biology teacher, is very helpful too. She is next door to you."

"Thanks. Actually, I need help now. Look at this schedule. Plus, I am expected to run the Science Club. I haven't even taught my first class and I am overwhelmed."

John sat in one of the student seats. He tapped his fingers gently on the desk. For some reason his long, outstretched legs, covered with brown pants, reminded Ann of logs.

He fixed his dark eyes on her and began to speak in a loud whisper. "It is truly a demanding schedule. Linda and I knew about it but were instructed not to say anything during the interview. The administrators were anxious to fill this science position and wanted it to look as appealing as possible."

"I see. What do you suggest that I do?"

"If you want to keep the job, you should look happy and do your best. I am also teaching some sections of Earth Science. To help you out, I will share some of my lessons and lab activities with you."

"I sincerely appreciate and accept your offer. Thanks!"

"In the remaining few minutes before class starts, let me show you where the ladies room and the teachers lounge are located."

Ann's spirits were lifted. She happily walked away with John. He seemed like a nice, caring person—one she could count on in time of need.

It was sixth period already. To Ann's surprise, the day was moving quickly and smoothly. So far all of the students were quiet and well-behaved. Maybe that was because she didn't know them and they didn't know her. Now Ann felt good about herself. She had successfully taught a general science class, a physical science class, and two chemistry classes. Actually, she distributed textbooks, stacked by subject in piles on her desk, to the students. After introducing herself to each class, she told the students to read part of the first chapter in the book and then they discussed it.

At the end of the fifth period, Linda Ames, the biology teacher, escorted her to the teachers lunchroom where they had a quick bite to eat. While there, she was introduced to the librarian, Marion, a matronly looking woman with a squeaky voice and glasses. She also met the two music teachers, Tom, the band conductor, and Pat, the chorus director.

Ann played show and tell with her students in the sixth period chemistry lab. She talked about lab safety and pointed out the location of safety goggles, the fire extinguisher, and the eyewash station.

Laboratory Safety Rules

1. *Know the location and use of safety equipment in the lab.*

2. *Follow the safety rules prepared by your teacher.*

3. *Read all directions and information on the Material Safety Data Sheets before beginning an investigation.*

4. *Wear safety goggles and other required protective attire.*

5. *Work in a supervised laboratory.*

6. *Be cautious and careful throughout the experiment.*

7. *Properly dispose of unused chemicals.*

8. *Clean up after each activity.*

While pointing to a chart of safety rules hanging on the wall next to the opened door, Ann noticed Mr. Jones standing there with his bright blue eyes fixed on her. Puzzled by his presence, she told the students to silently read the rules. Then she quickly walked toward him.

"I want you to meet me in my office at the end of the day."

Before she could respond, he was gone.

It was 3:30 p.m. Ann had just taught seven classes and was exhausted from standing and talking all day. She took a deep breath and knocked on the principal's door.

"Come in," he called in an unenthused voice.

Ann entered and the door noisily closed behind her.

At first glance, the room seemed bright and cheerful. Landscape paintings were beautifully displayed on the walls and colorful plants hung from the ceiling and adorned the bookshelves. The sun's rays, which entered through the rear window of the office, lit up the area and revealed the air's numerous dust particles.

Dressed in a black suit and seated behind a desk, his black dress shoes resting on a footstool, he looked like Count Dracula. She judged him to be about thirty years old. He was handsome even though his front teeth protruded a bit. In the sunlight, his thick head of curly blond hair shined intensely and his sparkling blue eyes took on a hypnotic glow.

"How was your first day of school?"

"It went well. Thanks."

"Good," he replied and then remained silent.

Not knowing what to say, Ann commented on one of his displays. "That is a very nice painting. I like the stream of blue water surrounded by pretty red and yellow flowers and the lifelike wildlife."

"It isn't really a nice painting. I just hung it there to cover the empty wall."

"Oh."

"Do you know why I asked you to come and see me?" He was on his feet as quickly as a predator springs on its prey.

"No, I don't," replied Ann in an uncertain voice. She was still standing in front of the closed door suffering silently with aching feet. Mr. Jones didn't even offer her a seat, even though two were available. She walked forward a few yards. Mr. Jones immediately backed up. Ann again strode ahead and Mr. Jones retreated.

I guess he doesn't want to be within four feet of me, she thought. She remained in place.

Mr. Jones proceeded with a monologue about an upcoming science event. Ann, who felt brain-dead by now, tuned out most of what he said. However, the punch line came through loud and clear: she would be organizing and leading the special activity.

"Excuse me," interrupted Ann. "I don't have a watch on and have no idea what time it is. Do you?"

Taking a close look at his wristwatch, he replied, "Yes. It is 6:00."

"Really," screeched Ann in a frantic voice. "I have to run. I am late for a dinner appointment."

Ann quickly gathered her belongings and raced out of the building.

It was 6:30 by the time Ann arrived at Bill Jackson's house for dinner. He had volunteered to prepare a candlelight dinner for two to celebrate her first day of teaching. She was one hour late.

"Where have you been?" Bill unhappily inquired. "I have been waiting for you and even called your place several times."

In a defensive voice, Ann sincerely apologized. "I am so very sorry for being late, but I haven't been home yet. I drove here straight from school."

"Really?"

"Yes! The principal asked me to meet with him in his office at the end of the day. He rambled on and on until I interrupted him to ask for the time. When he said that it was 6:00, I told him that I was late for a dinner appointment and left immediately. That is the true story. As you can guess, I am tired and extremely hungry."

"I am sorry to hear that you had such a challenging first day at school. You need to relax."

He handed Ann a large glass of soda and sat down on the couch beside her. He put his arm around her and gave her a big hug.

"Wow! I needed that."

"You are in luck. I made chicken breast in barbecue sauce with baked potatoes and carrots. They have been kept warm in the oven at a very low temperature setting."

"That's great. Thanks a lot for waiting for me. I do appreciate it. You are such a sweetheart."

"Ann, you know that I love you," whispered Bill with a smile as he gave her a soft kiss on the cheek. "Besides, you are conscientious and reliable, so I knew you would show up sooner or later."

They enjoyed a delicious meal together and talked for several hours. Ann discussed her day in detail, while Bill briefly mentioned that his went well.

5
Several Weeks Later

Three weeks passed. Ann's classes were going well and her only encounters with the principal were waves in the hallway and brief nods. It was a Friday afternoon and Ann decided to relax in the teachers lounge before going home. The room was small but cheerful. It had bright yellow curtains, several wooden chairs, a comfortable couch with a coffee table in front of it, and a microwave oven. Baked goods, deliciously displayed on the coffee table, caught Ann's attention. She never could resist sweets. While extending her arm to grab a jelly donut, she heard a voice call out behind her.

"I wouldn't eat those if I were you," said John Smith with a crazy laugh.

Startled, she turned around to face him.

"Why?"

"Let me tell you a little secret." He made himself comfortable on the couch and motioned her to sit down next to him. Once she was seated, he began to talk. "None of the teachers know it, but I come in here when the room is empty and lick all of the donuts."

"Really?"

"Oh, yes," he said in an excited voice. "I play this game once a week when we have our Friday sweets. It is very entertaining for me. I really enjoy watching people eat the donuts."

Ann looked at John with a straight face and spoke in a neutral voice. She was afraid to let him know that she thought he was weird and disgusting. After all, he was her mentor.

"Thanks for telling me your secret. I don't need a donut anyway. It will only ruin my supper."

"Ann, I like you and wouldn't want to do anything that would hurt you."

His coal-black eyes took on a glow as they sparkled at her.

Ann felt embarrassed and tried to prevent the color from rising in her cheeks. To her surprise, she bravely asked him another question.

"Do you have any other odd forms of entertainment?"

"Actually, I do. I will share one more secret with you if you promise not to tell."

"Okay."

"There is a substitute teacher at the school who loves food. Whenever he comes in, I obtain unwanted food items from teachers in the cafeteria. I make the food look pleasing to the eye and then offer it to him. Watching him wolf it down is quite a thrill. It is rather ironic. He thinks I am a nice guy because I give him free food."

"Wow! That is quite a story."

"It is true. You better keep your promise and not tell on me."

"I will," she assured him.

Ann felt awful on the inside. She hoped it didn't show on the outside. Here was a person she couldn't trust. She had better not cross him either.

"Well, I hate to run, but I am singing at the nursing home tonight. See you later."

Before she could get up from the couch, John gently grabbed her hand.

In a soft voice, he said, "Have a good evening."

He quickly left the room.

The next day at school, Ann kept a low profile and avoided John. She did make a special effort to speak to Linda Ames, the biology teacher next door to her.

"Hi!" Ann said as she stood at Linda's classroom door. "May I talk to you for a few minutes?"

"Certainly. Come in," replied Linda, who was alone and seated at a large wooden desk grading papers. "How is everything going? I have been so busy that I haven't had a chance to stop by to see you. I am truly sorry about that. If there is anything I can do to help you out, please let me know."

"Thanks. I appreciate the offer. So far the classes are okay. I was wondering if you could give me some general information and advice about this school and how it operates."

"That is a loaded request," chuckled the heavyset woman. She quickly rose out of her chair and closed the door. "I will warn you about the administration. In case you haven't noticed, there are few female teachers in this school. I believe that the administrators dislike women. My guess is that they gave you the job because they couldn't find a male applicant to fill the position."

"Are you serious?"

"Yes. They have even tried to get me to quit. Every time they do something mean, I file a grievance against them. So far I have been here for twelve years, but it hasn't been smooth sailing. Now they are trying to get rid of Miss Barns. Miss Barns is an excellent English teacher who has the room at the end of the hall. The students love her, and she is involved in many extracurricular activities."

"Why would they want to get rid of Miss Barns?"

"I think that they want to replace her with a man. They are saying that she made her students read an inappropriate book as a grounds to dismiss her. However, I don't think they will win their case."

"What do you suggest that I do as a new teacher?"

"I recommend that you don't rock the boat and try your best to please them. Remember, if you need anything, I am just next door. Hope you don't mind, but I am running late. These tests have to be graded by next period." She held the pile of exams in her fat hands and shook them in front of Ann's face.

"Oh, I don't mind." Ann opened the door to leave. "Thanks for your time and for the up-front information. Good luck with your paperwork."

Before returning to the classroom, Ann checked her mailbox in the main office. She had one piece of mail, a memo from the principal. It was handwritten on school letterhead. She read it immediately.

Please meet me in my office at the end of the day. I have something important to discuss with you.

Mike Jones, Principal

"Miss Philips, please have a seat," said Mr. Jones as he closed the office door and pointed to a wooden straight-back chair to the left of his desk.

"Thank you," replied Ann in a nervous voice. All day she had dreaded this meeting, especially after her conversation with Linda Ames.

"How is everything going?" He slowly looked her over with his large blue eyes.

"Fine."

Her cheeks felt like they were on fire. She lowered her eyes and quickly glanced over her outfit. She was decent.

"Some of your chemistry students have dropped in to see me. They say your pace for the course is too fast and that you are giving too much homework. The next thing you know, the parents will be calling up with complaints. We don't want that to happen, do we?" he asked with a twisted grin. "I suggest that you slow down and cut the amount of homework."

"I didn't realize this was a problem. The students haven't really said anything to me. They have grumbled a bit, but I didn't take them seriously. I will certainly do my best to accommodate them. However, the pace can't be modified very much if we are to cover all the material required for the chemistry regents."

"I hope that you do your best. As you can guess, I want my students to feel comfortable and to do well in the course. Maybe you could count a homework assignment like a unit test. That would make the class happy."

"I understand but—"

She didn't get a chance to finish her sentence.

"Ms. Philips, I don't think you know what I am talking about," Mike shouted in a firm voice.

"Yes I do."

"Okay. Then tell me what I am talking about."

His body shifted in the blue cushioned swivel chair behind his desk so that his eyes pierced hers. His face took on an expression of hate.

"I, uh . . . uh . . ."

There was a moment of silence, which seemed like an eternity to Ann. She was speechless and didn't know what to say. She would burst into tears if he yelled at her again.

Composing herself as best she could, Ann replied in a trembling voice, "I am to make the students happy and at the same time teach them all the material necessary to do well on the chemistry regents."

"That's right. Now you understand me." His voice toned down a bit.

"Yes."

"Good!" A forced smile came to his face. "The other item we need to discuss is the Science Club. As you already know, you are in charge of it. The third Wednesday in October is Invention Night. Each member of the Science Club will display and demonstrate his or her invention to parents and other interested members of the community. The event will be held in the school cafeteria. Any questions?"

"What do you expect me to do?"

He began a mirthless laugh. Ann fell silent.

"I expect you to do everything that needs to be done. Go ask your mentor, Mr. Smith, for advice. He ran the club last year."

"Okay."

"That's all for now. See you later."

Ann took his cue and left immediately.

It was first period Tuesday morning, a free period for Ann and John. Ann unwillingly knocked on John's closed door. She needed information for Invention Night. To her surprise, a student answered and told Ann that she caught Mr. Smith at a bad time.

"What do you mean?"

"He ripped his pants and quickly left the room dragging along his lab coat," replied the student.

"Where is he?"

"I think he is sitting in the lounge waiting for a teacher to mend his pants."

"Thanks!"

More out of curiosity than anything else, Ann quietly peeked in the teachers lounge. She saw John seated on the couch with his back to the door. He was wearing a lab coat. Luckily, he didn't notice her. She would talk to him at another time.

That evening Ann went out to dinner with Bill. They were at the new steakhouse in town. It had previously been called the Spaghetti Barrel, which closed because of poor business. The new owners remodeled the restaurant and hired some talented chefs from out of state.

Thank goodness the meal was delicious. Ann certainly needed something positive to boost her spirits. She ordered her favorite entree of prime rib, garlic mashed potatoes, and green beans.

Everything was cooked to perfection.

"My honey-roasted chicken is good. How is your food?" inquired Bill in a sweet voice.

"Oh, it is wonderful, just like you. Thanks for bringing me here tonight. The setting is so romantic and peaceful. We are eating by candlelight in a beautiful new restaurant with soft piano music in the background."

"You're welcome. I am happy that you are so pleased with my dinner suggestion. It is a celebration of us getting together again. I haven't seen much of you lately. You have been preoccupied with work, lesson plans, and extracurricular activities, like singing at the nursing home."

"I am sorry that I haven't had much time for you. I want you to know that you are more important to me than work and my other activities."

"Thank you for telling me that. I was beginning to think that you had found a new flame."

"Oh, Bill, I couldn't do that. It would take at least five guys to replace you."

"Wow! That is the ultimate compliment. Now that we are finished eating, let's burn up some calories by walking the three-mile trail behind this restaurant."

"That sounds like a good idea to me. I need the exercise and some fresh air too."

Thinking to herself, Ann decided the walk would be an excellent opportunity for her to discuss the school situation with Bill.

They held hands and strolled along the black top path, which surrounded a community golf course. They exchanged laughs and hugs, and periodically watched for fly balls. Birds singing and the aroma of wildflowers filled the air.

They were the only couple on the path. Ann stopped walking. She pulled Bill toward her and gave him a big hug. He closed his eyes and cherished the moment.

"Bill, thanks for the wonderful time tonight. I wish it would last forever." Pulling away from him, she continued. "I desperately need your advice."

"What do you mean?" he asked in a serious voice.

"My teaching job is turning into a nightmare."

"I am very sorry to hear that. What's the matter?"

"For starters, the principal yelled at me yesterday. He upset me so that I almost burst into tears. He rudely informed me that the students think my course is too difficult. He wants me to water down the chemistry to make the students happy. If I do that, the class won't be prepared for the regents. What should I do?"

"Have you talked to the other science teachers about it?"

"No, but I have talked to them. Unfortunately, they are rather weird. This morning the physics teacher was sitting in the teachers lounge in a lab coat waiting for his pants to be mended. I also know some other odd things about him, which I promised not to tell. The biology teacher told me that the administrators hate women and are trying to replace the female teachers with males. She isn't too bad, but she keeps to herself."

"This situation isn't good. However, I am not entirely surprised. The events that took place during your interview seemed strange to me. It isn't going to help by talking about the past. We need to address the problem at hand."

The sun was going down, so they resumed their walk at a quicker pace.

"I suggest that you hang in there a little longer and try your best to please them. If that doesn't work, you can always give one month's notice and quit. It isn't the end of the world. There are other jobs available. Please be happy, even if it is only because we will be engaged in a few months."

Ann paused and smiled. "I am happy because I am with you."

6
Dinner Date

"How are you doing? It's been a while since we talked to each other," said John as he walked into Ann's classroom during her free period.

"To tell you the truth, I could be better. Things aren't going well for me."

She decided to cautiously confide in John. After all, she needed his advice and assistance. She closed the door and sat in one of the student chairs. She looked pretty in her green silk suit.

Her eyes took on a special sparkle as she spoke. "The principal thinks my chemistry course is too hard. He wants me to water it down. Also, I am in charge of Invention Night. I found these interesting activities, but I don't really know what to do."

Inventions

1. Healthy Cookies

Students obtain a cookie recipe and modify it to prepare healthier cookies. For example, a cookie recipe requiring one-half cup of vegetable oil and two eggs could be modified to one-fourth cup of oil, one-fourth cup of water, and one egg. (Hint: Reducing the amount of eggs and oil lowers the fat and cholesterol in one's diet.)

Experiment with the recipe to invent a good-tasting cookie that is better for one's health. Write down the new recipe and share it with the class.

2. Strong Boat

Obtain several pieces of aluminum foil (12 inches by 12 inches/30 centimeters by 30 centimeters). Use each sheet to design a boat that will hold many pennies while floating in a plastic container of water. Test your boats. Which boat design holds the most pennies while floating in water? How many pennies does it hold? Share your boat invention with the class.

"I can help you out with Invention Night," said John. "However, you have to promise to have dinner with me tonight. That way we can discuss everything at length in a relaxed atmosphere."

"That sounds like a good deal to me. Thanks for your offer."

"How about we meet in the school parking lot at 4:30?"

"Okay. It's a date. See you later."

Ann made a special effort to smile and speak in an upbeat manner. She didn't want John to know what she really thought about him because she desperately needed his assistance.

To Ann's surprise the day was over before she knew it. Overall it was pleasant except for two distant encounters in the hall with the principal. He didn't speak to her, but hate was written all over his face.

Ann leisurely cleaned up the lab, putting away chemicals and equipment used in her chemistry activity on chemical reactions. Then she filled her briefcase with student homework papers, her gradebook, and a science book on inventions. Now she was ready to meet John in the parking lot.

The fresh air felt great. Ann hadn't been outside since early morning. It was cool and drizzly then. Now it was bright and sunny. She daydreamed about the nice weather and beautiful scenery as she walked to her car. Within inches of the car, her daydream ended.

"Oh my goodness!" she screamed.

Two of the car's tires had been slashed. The left front and back tires were as flat as pancakes.

"What's wrong?" asked John as he approached her from behind.

"Look at my car. What am I going to do?"

"Calm down. Don't worry. I will take care of everything. People usually think better on a full stomach. Why don't you put the briefcase in your car and lock it up? I will drive us to the restaurant and then help you with your car."

Ann, who was in a semi-shocked state, automatically did as told and hopped into his car. She was speechless for several moments. John immediately started the car and drove out of the parking lot.

Finally managing to speak in a weak voice she said, "You are probably right. Thanks."

Ann thought to herself. *How can someone so weird act so nice?*

John gently touched her shoulder and said, "Everything will be fine. Just relax.

To relieve your mind of the current problem, I will share today's entertainment with you. However, you must again promise not to tell anyone. It is our little secret."

"Okay," said Ann as she turned her head to face him. She had been looking out the front windshield and was only half-listening to his words. Her mind was elsewhere.

"Have you met Ms. Jacobs, the Social Studies teacher on the first floor?"

"I don't think so. What does she look like?"

"She is a large woman and slow moving. She must be in her mid-fifties, wears glasses, and has shoulder length, grayish-blonde hair. The students don't really like her, and in my opinion she is a poor teacher. She teaches four periods in a row and is usually thirsty after her third class. Unfortunately, she is quite far from a water fountain; therefore, she appreciates it that once a week I supply her with a drink. Actually, I have a reliable student deliver it to her. The catch is that the drinks are diverse and range from ice water to slightly soured milk. My student watches her gulp down the liquid. Then he returns the glass to me with a vivid description of the event. Periodically, Ms. Jacobs thanks me for my thoughtfulness. I really enjoy this game," he said with a devilish grin.

"Oh," replied Ann in a monotone trying to keep her inner feelings a secret. Actually, John succeeded in making her feel worse instead of better. She didn't want him to know that. After all, he was taking her to dinner and offered to help with the car. She needed to keep a positive frame of mind. Ann immediately changed the topic of conversation.

"How much longer will it take us to get to the restaurant?"

"We should be there in about ten minutes or so. I like you, Ann, and always look forward to our moments together. I hope that you are enjoying your ride with me."

"Oh yes. The company and scenery are fine."

"Good. I will use this time to help you get to know me better."

While driving down an old country road, they saw trees and wild-flowers and passed farms with cows and horses grazing in green pastures. It appeared to be a lovely day that was picturesque and peaceful. Ann continued to face John as he spoke.

"I grew up in this town and attended the school where we both work. I feel like part of the building's foundation. My students wouldn't dare complain about my teaching, and they wouldn't think of giving me a hard time. They know what happens when I lose my temper. I guess you could say that I turn into a beast," he bellowed as he shot a wild grin at Ann. "My father can be thanked for that. He always beat me when I was growing up. If I displeased him in any way, he would torture me. One time when I got in trouble in seventh grade for not having my assignments done, he tied me up with rope and burned me with a cigarette."

"Oh, that is terrible! I am sorry that you have been treated so cruelly by your father."

"I managed to survive. However, now I tend to be mean to people who annoy or bother me. I would never be mean to you, Ann," he said sweetly.

John made a right-hand turn onto a narrow dirt road, barely wide enough for one car. He was driving into a wooded area.

"Where are we?" inquired Ann in a puzzled voice.

"This is a shortcut to the restaurant. I know all the back roads by heart. We are almost there."

"Which restaurant are we going to?"

"I can't tell you because I want it to be a surprise. Hold on."

He quickly stepped on the accelerator and the car leaped forward.

John, who was driving very fast down a narrow dirt road, successfully dodged numerous rocks and holes. Ann was bouncing around in her seat. Thanks to a seatbelt, she didn't hit her head on the car's ceiling or slam hard into the door. The tall canopy of maple trees lining both sides of the path-like road served as an umbrella for them. The ride resembled a roller coaster speeding through a tunnel of trees. Ann didn't like fast rides. They made her feel sick.

Feeling queasy and upset, she screamed, "Slow down!"

"Do you think this is too slow and want me to drive faster?"

"No!"

"I'm only joking." John slowed down a bit. "I just wanted to give you a joy ride. It's like being at the amusement park together. I find it exciting and thought you would too."

"Please stop the car. I feel sick."

John pulled over to the side of the narrow dirt road. Fortunately, his car was the only one on it. As he carefully helped Ann, who was as pale as a ghost, out of the passenger seat, she collapsed into his arms.

―――――――――――――――――――――――――

The nightmare began. Ann felt cool and confined. She had to be very quiet so the guys wouldn't find her. She lay flat on her back in a drainage ditch that was about two feet deep. Staring up at the star-lit sky, she could detect the glare of the car's headlights searching for her.

Just moments ago she had been walking alone in the dark, when the swerving car appeared. Its drunk occupants were rowdy and threw an object at her. Then they drove away. Anticipating their possible return, Ann desperately ran to a nearby house, with a semicircular driveway. Screaming for help, she frantically banged on a door of the dark, secluded home sheltered by trees. No one answered. Turning away to face the road, she saw the detested car approaching. Ann stumbled behind tall shrubs and trees looking for a place to hide. With no time to spare, she quickly jumped into the ditch.

The motor stopped and male voices, using slurred speech, filled the air.

"Where did the gal go?"

"I don know, Bruce. She can't be far. We just saw her."

"Search the area, Todd, while I circle the driveway with the car."

Ann knew she would soon be discovered. To calm her nerves, she held a silent conversation with herself about positive memories from the past. However, a bright flashlight shining inches above her face brought Ann back to reality.

"*Help!*" she screamed at the top of her lungs. "They are after me."

"Ann, you are okay. It must be a bad dream," said John in a soothing voice as he removed the flashlight from her view.

She tried to move, but he laid a restraining hand on her shoulder and said, "Better lie still a bit longer."

Ann realized she was lying on the grass. "How did I get here?" she asked, not remembering exactly what happened.

"I carried you here after you fainted in my arms."

"Oh, I thought . . ." She started to sit up.

"Ann, I tried my best to help you."

"How long have we been here?"

"I don't really know. I have lost track of the time."

Ann stood up but felt a bit unsteady. Suddenly, John was standing beside her. He put her hand in his and gently squeezed it.

"Please believe what I told you."

It was getting dark and she was alone in the woods with John.

There wasn't much she could say. "I believe you, John," she replied in an apologetic voice.

"Good, because I love you. My heart sank the first time I saw you."

He quickly put his arms around her and gave her the biggest hug ever. Ann turned red with embarrassment. She was breathless and unable to get away from him. John swept Ann off her feet and twirled her around and around in circles in a romantic frenzy. Her head was spinning as she faded away into oblivion.

7
Missing

Bill felt uneasy and sensed that something was wrong. He had been calling Ann for several days now and she still wasn't home or at least didn't answer the phone. That wasn't like Ann. She usually told him in advance if she was going to be busy for a long stretch of time. He would give her the benefit of the doubt.

Who knows, maybe her phone is out of order, Bill thought.

He decided to drive over to her place. It was 9:00 on a Friday evening. Ann's place was dark. Her car was gone. He tried the door, but found it locked. Mail was in the mailbox. He couldn't tell if it was just today's mail or several days' worth.

He cruised around town in his car thinking.

Maybe Ann has a new boyfriend and doesn't have the heart to tell me. After all, she is very attractive. She might be out with some friends or is keeping busy with extracurricular activities. When it comes to volunteer work, Ann has a hard time saying no.

He would call her parents tonight. If that proved to be fruitless, he would call her school on Monday if necessary.

"Hello, Mrs. Philips. This is Bill. How are you?"

"I'm fine. How are you doing?"

"Okay. Have you heard from Ann lately?"

"Not in about a week or so. She seems to be very busy with that job of hers. I hope that both of you still plan to come down for Thanksgiving. We look forward to seeing you again. Ann's brothers will be here too. It should be fun."

"Oh yes. We will be there. I wouldn't miss your delicious cooking for the world." Not wanting to alarm Ann's mother, Bill decided to keep the conversation short. "Well, I just called to say hello. Give my best wishes to Mr. Philips and the family. Take care and we will see you soon. Good-bye."

"Good-bye Bill."

Monday arrived and still no word from Ann. Bill dialed the phone number to her school during his preparation period.

"I am very sorry, Mr. Jackson. Ann hasn't been in for several days. A substitute is teaching her classes," said the school secretary in a sincere voice.

"I am her boyfriend, soon to be fiancé and haven't heard from her in days. Do you know if she is at a conference or at home sick?"

"I don't know anything about her except that she hasn't been in school for several days."

"I am worried about her. Is there anyone else whom I can talk to?"

"Not really. Right now the principal and superintendent are in a meeting. Maybe I can find out something and get back to you."

"Thanks for the offer, but I guess it would be better for me to stop by after school. Do you think the principal would be able to meet with me at 3:30 today?"

"Hold on a minute, Mr. Jackson. Let me check his schedule." She put Bill on hold and ran into the principal's office to inform him of the situation. He immediately picked up the telephone.

"Hello, Mr. Jackson. I'm Mike Jones, the high school principal. I understand that you are concerned about Miss Philips."

"Yes, I am worried about her. Do you have any information for me?"

"I have a little bit. As you must know, we also care about Miss Philips. Up until now we have given her situation a low profile, so as not to upset the students and her fellow teachers. We know that she had car trouble last Wednesday and that one of our teachers gave her a ride to a nearby gas station to obtain help. Unfortunately, she hasn't been seen or heard from since."

"Where is this gas station located?"

"It is about one mile past our school on the left. You can't miss it."

"Thank you very much for your time and information. I appreciate it."

"Sorry I can't be more helpful. Please let me know if you find out anything more," Mike said in a serious voice.

"I will. Thanks again. Good-bye."

"Good-bye."

Ann partially opened her eyes. She found herself looking around a small moon-lit room. She felt dizzy but realized that she was in a strange bed still dressed in her clothes. Her thoughts quickly drifted to Bill. If only he were here. She recalled his face to fill the room's black void. Ann dozed off dreaming about Bill. It was a sunny day and they were strolling hand in hand through a beautiful flower garden filled with exotic birds and pleasing smells. They were laughing and exchanging pleasant stories.

Suddenly, Ann awoke with a start. Someone was hovering over her. The daylight clearly showed a creature draped in a black cape wearing a vampire mask and black gloves. She screamed!

"Come to me," he said in a muffled voice. He quickly grabbed Ann and shook her shoulders. "Soon you will be mine." His face came brutally down on hers.

"*No!*" she cried.

"How dare you deny me!"

Ann suddenly lost her balance and fell to the floor.

"I hope that you will be in a better mood when I return."

He slammed the door and disappeared from sight.

After what seemed like hours of crying, Ann pulled herself together. She ran to the door but it was locked and wouldn't budge. Then she eyed sandwiches and juice on a small wooden table in front of the bed. She hadn't eaten in hours. Without even thinking, she wolfed down everything.

The room wasn't very big, but fortunately it included a bathroom. Even though she would be wearing the same clothes, Ann decided to bathe. She locked the bathroom door and took a quick shower using the shampoo and hand soap that she found in the stall. She dried herself off with a shabby grey towel and got dressed. She felt somewhat refreshed and hoped that her brain cells were stimulated.

Ann seriously studied the view through a window next to her bed. Tall trees were everywhere.

"I must escape from here," she whispered to herself.

Darkness came quickly, so she crawled into bed for the night.

Bill was highly upset and frustrated. Days passed by and still no word from or about Ann. He did everything he could think of. He called the village police and reported her as a missing person. He even broke down and called Ann's parents again but assured them that everything would be okay.

It was Wednesday afternoon, exactly one week after Ann's disappearance. Bill managed to mechanically teach his chemistry classes, almost without realizing it, because he was so deep in thought about Ann. He taught a lesson about chemical bonds. Actually, the students really enjoyed it.

Chemical Bond Activity

First Bill told the students that they use tape and glue to hold things together in their daily lives. He mentioned that chemicals are held together by bonds. Covalent bonds are made by the sharing of electrons, while ionic bonds are made by the attraction of oppositely charged ions.

Then his students used various items such as gum, candy, and rubber bands to simulate the stretching of bonds. They measured and recorded the original length of each item in centimeters. Next they stretched each item up to its breaking point (just before it breaks). Again they measured and recorded the length of each stretched item. It was interesting to note the item that stretched the most.

Bill decided to visit the gas station near the school where Ann taught.

The old, senile owner of the dilapidated gas station said, "To tell you the truth, people come and go so often that I rarely notice anyone. I wish that I could help you but ..."

"Please give me a couple more minutes," Bill pleaded desperately. "My Ann is missing. I was told that she was dropped off here last Wednesday. Apparently, she had car trouble and needed assistance. She is attractive, so I think you would have noticed her. She is a short, slim, well-built woman with long brown hair and bright brown eyes."

"The sight of her would have brightened my day," he replied with a smile. "Unfortunately, I don't remember seeing her, although that may be due to my failing memory."

"Okay. Thanks for your time."

As Bill drove off, he noticed the school where Ann taught. He needed to talk to the teacher who supposedly dropped Ann off at the gas station.

Bill pulled into the school parking lot. He got out of his car and slammed the door. It was then that he saw Ann's car (with its flat tires) parked nearby.

"Oh my goodness," he cried. In a flash he was standing in the school's main office, demanding to speak to the teacher who assisted Ann.

"Please be seated, Mr. Jackson," said a pleasant secretary with white hair, glasses, and a soft smile. "Mr. John Smith, our physics teacher, will be with you in a moment."

"Thank you."

Before Bill had a chance to sit down, Mr. Smith appeared. The friendly secretary introduced the teachers to each other.

"I understand that you gave Ann a ride to the nearby gas station last Wednesday!" blurted out Bill emotionally.

John Smith spoke slowly in a serious and concerned voice. "That is true. I told Ann that I would help her. She was very upset about her car. The tires looked like they had been slashed. To make a long story short, I gave her a lift at the end of the school day to the nearby gas station. Actually, I dropped her off in front of it, because I had an important errand to run. I told her about it and said that I would be back in twenty minutes. She nodded her head in agreement. Then I left. Unfortunately, that was the last time I saw her. When I returned, she was gone. I assumed that she caught a ride home with someone."

"I see," whispered Bill. "Then what . . . ?"

"As I told you before, I thought Ann was okay. However, when she didn't show up for work on Thursday, I panicked and immediately informed the principal of the situation. We contacted the police and solicited leads to her whereabouts. Personally, I think she may have been picked up by someone. Maybe she was standing in front of the gas station and was offered a ride. Who knows? There is nothing more that I can say."

"I understand. Thanks a lot for the information," answered Bill in a controlled voice. He said good-bye and left.

Ann wearily sat on her bed scanning the sunlit room. Her eyes focused on five bricks piled in a corner. A car motor broke her trance. Then came the sound of loud footsteps. Ann braced herself. Suddenly, the door flew open and the creature dressed as Dracula entered.

"I brought you something," he said in a muffled voice. He carefully placed some food and juice on the small table. "Come to me!"

Ann took a deep breath and slowly moved toward him. He was tall and completely dressed in black. A vampire mask with protruding teeth and dripping blood covered his head. Ann bravely let her eyes meet his.

Dracula attempted to put his hands on her arms. She flinched in anticipated pain.

"Don't you like me?" he shouted angrily.

"Ahh . . ." her lips trembled.

He stepped back and clenched his hand into a fist. "That answer means *no!* I thought you were special and that we could get married. You are making me angry. I must teach you a lesson."

Ann's cheeks filled with color and her eyes swelled with tears.

"I'm sorry," she answered in a forced voice.

"It is too late for sorry!"

Ann swung around and ran into the bathroom. She immediately locked the door.

"Come out of there!" he demanded.

Ann remained silent and pressed her body against the wooden door.

"Oh, I see. You want to play hide and seek." Dracula burst into mirthless laughter. "I must go now, but when I return, you will play my game."

Ann remained in the bathroom until her captor drove away. She devoured the food that he had left on the table. She was very hungry and could hear her stomach growling.

Ann tried to open the main door, but it was locked again and wouldn't budge.

"I must get out of here!" she said in a determined voice as she hugged herself.

She faced the window and tried to force it open. Nothing happened. Maybe it was glued shut.

"Think! Think!" she shouted to herself.

Ann was at least twenty feet above the ground. She eyed the bricks. One by one she threw four of them each at different sections of the window. Luckily, the glass shattered. She used the fifth brick to smooth the inner edge of the window frame and to remove the remaining sharp pointed glass fragments. She worked as quickly as possible.

She stripped the bed of its bedspread and sheets, cautiously shaking each one to assure the absence of glass, and then she tied them all together to form a long rope.

Ann easily moved the bed next to the window and carefully tied her self-made rope to its bedpost. Thanks to her experience on the high school gymnastics team, she was prepared to maneuver this rope.

She stood on the bed and wrapped the rope around her leg. Cautiously, Ann squeezed her body through the window opening, avoiding any remaining glass. Surrounded by tall trees, she slowly lowered herself down the rope of bedding.

Within minutes she was standing on the ground in front of a two story cabin.

"I made it!" sighed Ann as she quickly walked along a dirt path that led away from her prison.

Time was passing. Ann listened intently. There were no cars nearby, but her captor could return at any moment. She decided to walk in the thick wooded area parallel to the dirt path. It would be longer and more labored, but at least she would be hidden from view. Her feet and legs ached and she was thoroughly exhausted. She fought a huge wave of weariness that seemed to engulf her.

Ann always loved the woods and spent many hours there as a child. To offset her awful physical condition, she imagined herself picking blackberries and playing house in a tree fort with her younger siblings. Her woods, as she often called them, were peaceful and very beautiful with flowing brook and fragrant flowers.

Ann felt faint. Weakness overtook her body as she gracefully collapsed under a maple tree.

The police car pulled up to the school. Officer Art Thomas got out. He walked over to Ann's car and closely examined the tires.

"Yeah, Principal Jones, these tires were probably slashed with a knife," he said briskly. "Did you find a knife or any tools in the parking lot?"

"No! Unfortunately, we have found nothing, but as you must know we are very concerned about Ann."

"Did anyone notice anything strange or unusual in the parking lot on the day of the incident? It is possible that whoever is responsible for the tire damage may also be involved in Ann's disappearance."

"That may be true," responded Principal Jones in a serious voice. "However, it could have been just a prank played on her by an irate student."

"What do you mean by that?" Art's hand was in his pocket now. He was jiggling his change. It was a nervous habit that he had since childhood.

"Well, shortly before her disappearance, some students came to my office complaining about Miss Philip's teaching. They said that her course was too hard. Students at our school sometimes display rash behavior when they are upset."

"Really!"

"Oh yes!" exclaimed the principal as he became wide-eyed and animated. "There was the incident when Mr. Jenkin's science lab was literally turned into a fountain. By the way, he no longer teaches at this school. Mr. Jenkins was an odd-looking character with bowed legs, bushy eyebrows, and a big nose. Everyone teased him." He chuckled. "Anyway, an angry student who served in-school suspension because of him entered the empty lab and unscrewed the faucets and water spouts. You can imagine the terrible shock of starting a class in a room filled with jets of spraying water."

"*Wow!*"

Bill was lovesick and very weary. He couldn't sleep or eat well since Ann's disappearance. She was constantly on his mind. He loved her very much and wished that he could hold and comfort her now. So far there was no information as to her whereabouts. He was helpless and didn't know which way to turn. His only hope was the science teacher, John Smith, who supposedly gave Ann a ride to a nearby gas station. For no apparent reason, Bill had a deep inner feeling that this teacher was hiding something. He was determined to find out all he could to save his very wonderful and beautiful Ann. Soon he would pay Mr. Smith a visit.

Ann's captor noticed the approaching darkness as he drove down the secluded dirt road. She would be nice to him tonight. He knew that she really liked him, but he had been a bit harsh with her. This time he'd be patient so that she could enjoy his company.

He was so excited that he could hardly wait to see her. Ann's sparkling eyes and good looks were vivid in his mind. Tonight he would reveal his identity. He was wearing new blue slacks and a white dress shirt. "She will be very impressed with the handsome man behind the Dracula mask!" he shouted with an arrogant smile.

The driver brought his car to a screeching halt. He noticed the broken window with bedding dangling from it. Enraged, he charged into the cabin. Within seconds, he was in Ann's second story room screaming, "You will never escape from me!!"

He quickly walked through the cabin, grabbed a flashlight, and scrambled into the woods to search for Ann. He would find her if it was the last thing he ever did. She was his "everything."

The doorbell rang at 8:00 p.m. John Smith greeted his unexpected visitor in an agitated manner.

"What are you doing here?"

"May I please come in for just a minute?" Bill asked frantically. "I am Ann Philip's boyfriend. You must remember me from our meeting at the school."

"Yes, I do. Come in if you must."

Bill entered the house, closing the door behind him. He immediately blurted out his thoughts. "Ann's life may be in danger. You are the last person who remembers seeing her."

"How do you know that?" asked John in a concerned voice.

"I have my ways of finding out things," bluffed Bill. "If you help me rescue Ann, I will do my best to keep you out of trouble with the police. Is it a deal?"

John stood speechless, staring into space for several moments. Then he spoke slowly, as if in a trance. "I never thought about the cops. They might try to pin this crime on me and put me in jail." He became more animated. "It's all his fault. It was his idea. I like Ann and wouldn't do anything to harm her."

"Where is she?" shouted Bill. "Let's go there now before it is too late."

John, who seemed to have a sudden burst of energy, began to speak quickly and excitedly. "He said that he wanted her to stay at the cabin for a few days. That way he could teach her a lesson and talk to her privately without being disturbed. He assured me that she would be alright, although I don't really trust him."

Now John was upset and worried about Ann. In his heart, he knew that he loved her very much. He must do his best for her.

"Okay, Bill. I'll take you up on your offer and drive us out to the cabin."

Ann, who had been asleep under a maple tree, woke up startled. A bright light was shining in her face.

"Oh thank goodness you found me!"

She eagerly embraced the man squatting next to her. Then they both stood up. He cherished this unexpected sign of affection. He felt happy and pleased. Ann looked beautiful in the moonlight.

She glanced up at him. Her sparkling eyes bore through his. Excitement overtook him. His arms closed tightly around her. She struggled to get away. He went wild. Rejection always did this to him. To make matters worse, she had rejected his teaching ideas at school too.

He released her for a moment to retrieve his flashlight. She was free. Ann quickly filled her lungs with air and ran. Mike Jones was in hot pursuit. He would teach her a lesson she'd never forget.

"Look! That's Mike's car. They must be in the cabin."

John and Bill went up to the front door and knocked on it loudly. No one answered. After waiting a moment, John slowly opened the unlocked door. His eyes roved the area. Impatiently, he darted into the front room with Bill at his heels.

"Ann, Mike, are you in here?" John shouted excitedly.

No response.

Together the men called out the names again and again as they searched each room.

Still no response.

Finally, they grabbed flashlights from a kitchen pantry and ventured into the woods.

Ann didn't get far. She was weak and couldn't maneuver well in the dark. Her arms and legs were scratched and bruised from encounters with the unseen trees and bushes that surrounded her.

Her enemy was only a few yards away.

"Ow!" Ann screamed as she tripped over a broken branch and fell. Her twisted ankle throbbed with a deep, piercing pain. She was unable to get up.

"Now I have you. You won't get away this time!" roared Mike with mirthless laughter.

It was time to play the cat and mouse game. Of course, he was the cat and she was the injured mouse. He would play with her a bit before he killed her.

"Did you get hurt, my dearest Ann?" he inquired in a sarcastic voice.

Ann lay still, suffering in silence. Tears swelled up in her eyes.

"Answer me!" he demanded.

Crying aloud, Ann replied, "Yes. I hurt my leg."

"Do you expect me to help you?"

"Please help me, Mike," she begged while sobbing in a sweet voice. "I'm truly sorry if I offended you before. I didn't mean to. It's just that I was afraid of you and thought that you might hurt me. Actually, I really like you."

She had to lie a bit to stall for time and hopefully get his sympathy.

"You look handsome in that white dress shirt. I noticed it right away."

Maybe she really did like him. His previous actions may have frightened her. Now he was puzzled. He needed time to think. Because he really loved her, he would give Ann one more chance to prove her feelings for him.

"Darling, I will hold you in my arms to comfort you," he said sincerely.

"Thanks! That would be nice." She pretended to be pleased with his suggestion.

Ann snuggled in his arms with her head nestled close to his warm inviting chest. Despite the pain, she felt relaxed and secure. In her mind she was embraced by Bill, whom she loved very much.

Mike noticed how natural and peaceful Ann seemed in his arms. She really did love him. His fingers gently caressed her hair while his lips softly kissed the top of her head.

Bill was in deep thought as he lingered a considerable distance behind John in the dark wooded area. So far it had been a productive day. Thank God he remembered to phone the police before driving to John Smith's house. Yeah! He gave them exaggerated details and blew his suspicions out of proportion. But it was necessary. He needed cops to shadow his every movement this evening. Slowly turning his head sideways, Bill caught sight of the police escorts. He cautiously waved them ahead in John's direction.

Mike's romantic tranquility was suddenly disturbed. He heard crunching footsteps approaching and saw a light in the distance. Unconsciously, he placed Ann's relaxed body on the ground next to him and sprang to his feet. Mike's eyes searched for a place to hide. He spotted a large boulder and went over to it.

"Mike, Mike, where are you? I know you're out here," yelled John hysterically as he rambled on through the trees. "What have you done to Ann?"

After stumbling over several branches, he noticed Ann's motionless body sprawled out in front of him. John paused and stared for only a moment. Then he screamed and beat his chest like a wild beast. Immediately, he leaped forward in pursuit of Mike.

Mike was overwhelmed by the closeness of John's threatening voice. He stood up behind his shield of rock and looked him in the face. John slowed his pace.

"John, calm down! Ann is fine. She is just sleeping. We were having a wonderful time together, when I was frightened off by your approaching footsteps."

John moved with the swiftness of an animal striking its prey. He punched Mike in the face. In a moment both men were wrestling on the ground. John was the stronger of the two.

Police sirens filled the air. Cops were everywhere.

"Break it up guys. You are both under arrest," bellowed Sergeant Doyle in a firm voice. Two officers immediately handcuffed the men and escorted them to a patrol car.

Ann was famished and thoroughly exhausted. She must have easily dozed off in this cold dark place. The roar of sirens and rustling footsteps stirred her and brought her back to her senses. She pulled herself into a sitting position with her back snug against a tree. Wide-eyed she carefully scanned her surroundings.

"Ann, my darling, are you okay?" shouted Bill as he rushed to her side. "Thank goodness you are alive," he sighed with relief as he gently kissed her on the check. "I love you very much!"

The sight of Bill brought a big smile to Ann's face. Words alone could not express her happiness. "I am fine now that you have rescued me!" exclaimed Ann joyfully. "I love you too."

Ann and Bill embraced each other. It was truly a wonderful reunion and a moment that they both would cherish forever.

Chapter 3

Scientists solve problems by trying to find cause and effect relationships between seemingly unrelated data. In doing so, they ask good questions such as: What? When? Why? How?

Scientists conduct investigations with open-mindedness and curiosity. They follow a logical set of steps, which may vary from scientist to scientist. The following is a Problem-Solving Model:

Problem-Solving Model

1. Problem- One should be able to define the problem (that which needs to be solved).

2. Available Information- One should be able to record available information that pertains to the problem.

3. Other Needed Data- One should be able to list other required information needed to solve the problem.

4. Procedure to Obtain Needed Data- One should be able to prepare a set of steps or a procedure to obtain data to solve the problem.

5. Record the Data- One should be able to record or list the new data that pertains to the problem.

6. Organize the Data- One should be able to organize the data (ex. according to a similar property).

7. Analyze the Data- One should be able to analyze or closely study the data.

8. Generalize from the Data- One should be able to make generalizations or general statements from the data.

9. Decision Making- One should be able to make a decision and hopefully solve the problem.

At this point, have the students read the first seven parts of "Mail Mystery." Students should relate the Model for Problem Solving to the reading.

Chapter 4

After reading the first seven parts of "Mail Mystery," have the students do the following activity.

Assume you are a detective to solve the case in the story. You will prepare your report of the investigation by using the steps in the Problem-Solving Model.

Report of Investigation

1. Problem- Define what needs to be solved (Hint: the crime).

2. Available Information- Record all available information that pertains to the problem.

3. Other Needed Data- List the other required information needed to solve the problem.

4. Procedure to Obtain Needed Data- Prepare a set of steps or a procedure to obtain the data needed to solve the problem.

Have the students finish reading the short story. Then have them complete their Reports of Investigation.

5. Procedure to Obtain Needed Data- Describe the procedure used in the story to obtain the needed data.

6. Record the Data- Record or list the new data or information that pertains to the problem.

7. Organize the Data- Set up a chart of the data showing names, places, and motives.

8. Analyze the Data- Closely study all the data.

9. Generalize from the Data- After having studied the data, make some general statements.

10. Decision Making- Make a decision and solve the case (problem).

Chapter 5

(The thinking processes associated with science can be called "science skills").

Observing- Noting the properties of people, objects, and events by using one's senses.

Classifying- Grouping people, places, objects, ideas, or events into categories based on their similarities.

Using Numbers- Using quantitative relationships such as percents and proportions.

Measuring- Making quantitative observations.

Inferring- Giving explanations for a specific object or event.

Predicting- Making forecasts of future occurrences based on past observations.

Interpreting Data- Analyzing data to arrive at explanations.

Chapter 6

Bloom's Taxonomy of Cognitive Objectives contains six levels. The knowledge level represents the lowest level in the Taxonomy, and Evaluation represents the highest level. Questions from the lower levels require less thinking on the part of the learner than questions from the higher levels. Classroom teaching should include a mixture of lower level and higher level questions.

Knowledge - Memory, recall.

Comprehension - Understanding a concept or idea and being able to explain it in one's own words.

Application - Solve problems by applying rules.

Analysis - Subdivide something. Distinguish the parts from the whole.

Synthesis - Create or produce ideas or ways.

Evaluation - Judge, make value decisions.

Chapter 7

After reading the short story, "Mail Mystery," have the students use Science Process Skills to analyze it.

The following student activities are written in terms of behavioral objectives. Each activity is written at a specific level of learning and involves a specific Science Process Skill.

Science Process Skill   Level of Learning
Observing   Knowledge

Behavioral Objectives

1. The students should be able to list the main characters in the short story.

2. The students should be able to describe the main characters in the short story.

3. The students should be able to state where the story takes place.

4. The students should be able to state when this story takes place.

5. The students should be able to state where Sue Phillips lives.

Science Process Skill   Level of Learning
Classifying   Knowledge

Behavioral Objectives

1. The students should be able to list the characters who belong to the Phillips' family.

2. The students should be able to list the characters who work at the post office.

3. The students should be able to list the characters who are cops.

4. The students should be able to list the characters who are lawyers.

Science Process Skill	Level of Learning
Interpreting Data	Comprehension

Behavioral Objectives

1. The students should be able to explain what is meant by, "Going solo on a mail route."

2. The students should be able to explain what is meant by, "In our business, we can't take chances."

3. The students should be able to explain what is meant by, "I finally met someone more ingenious than myself."

Science Process Skill	Level of Learning
Measuring	Comprehension

Behavioral Objectives

1. The students should be able to estimate Sue Phillips' age. Explain.

2. The students should be able to estimate the amount of time involved in the short story. Explain.

Science Process Skill	Level of Learning
Using Numbers	Application

Behavioral Objectives

Assume that houses on the left side of a given street have even numbers and that houses on the right side have odd numbers.

1. One delivers mail only to the right side of the street starting with house #17 and ending with house #51. The students should be able to determine the number of houses that received mail.

2. One delivers mail to both sides of the street starting with house #17 and ending with house #51. The students should be able to determine the number of houses that received mail.

Science Process Skill
Inferring

Level of Learning
Analysis

Behavioral Objectives

1. Sue Phillips asked questions about dogs and wore wool pants to work. The students should be able to infer Sue's relationship to dogs.

2. Mr. Lawrence appeared tired and nervous at work the morning after Sue's disappearance. The students should be able to infer the reason for Mr. Lawrence's weary appearance.

3. The story mentions that Sergeant Miles almost single-handedly caught professional robbers in Rome. The students should be able to infer some attributes of Sergeant Miles' character.

Science Process Skill
Predicting

Level of Learning
Synthesis

Behavioral Objectives

1. The students should be able to create a short essay describing Sue Phillips' future after returning home from the hospital.

2. The students should be able to create a short essay describing the future of the criminals in the story (Hint: Will they be set free soon? If so, what will they do?).

Science Process Skill   Level of Learning
Interpreting Data   Evaluation

Behavioral Objectives

1. The students should be able to compare the characters Dan Phillips and James Brown. Discuss their similarities and differences.

2. The students should be able to support Joe's, James', and Dave's decision to silence Sue. List reasons in support of that decision.

3. The students should be able to criticize Joe's, James', and Dave's decision to silence Sue. List reasons that criticize that decision.

Chapter 8

The short story, "Mail Mystery," contains words that are related to science. These words have been developed into science discussions and activities that enhance one's knowledge of science and one's understanding of the words themselves.

a. Human Genetics

This topic has been developed from the following words: father, mother, children, brown eyes, blue eyes, and pattern baldness.

Human Genetics is the study of human heredity. It is the transmission of characteristics from parents to offspring. Inherited traits or characteristics are controlled by genes. Genes are distinct units of heredity. They are the physical basis for all traits of an individual. Each individual contains two genes (one from each parent) for each trait. If the two genes for a trait are alike, the individual is said to homozygous for the trait. If one gene of the pair masks the expression of the other, it is dominant and the masked gene is recessive. Recessive genes are only expressed when both genes of the pair are recessive. Dominant genes are represented by capital letters and recessive genes are represented by lowercase letters. The word "genotype" is used to describe the genes that an individual possesses. The word "phenotype" describes the individual's observable traits (ex. brown eye color).

Let's use a Punnett Square to visualize all the possible gene combinations for eye color that parents might give to their offspring.

Let B stand for the dominant brown eye color gene.

Let b stand for the recessive blue eye color gene.

Parent Genotype	Parent Phenotype
Bb	Brown Eyes
bb	Blue Eyes

Punnett Square

	B	b
b	bB	bb
b	bB	bb

Genotype of Offspring	Phenotype of Offspring
bB	Brown Eyes
bb	Blue Eyes
bB	Brown Eyes
bb	Blue Eyes

Predict the offspring's Genotype and Phenotype for eye color from the following parents.

Parent Genotype	Parent Phenotype
Bb	Brown Eyes
Bb	Brown Eyes

Punnett Square

	B	b
B		
b		

Genotype of Offspring	Phenotype of Offspring
_____	_____
_____	_____
_____	_____
_____	_____

Parent Genotype
BB
bb

Parent Phenotype
Brown Eyes
Blue Eyes

Punnett Square

	B	B
b		
b		

Genotype of Offspring

_____

_____

_____

_____

Phenotype of Offspring

_____

_____

_____

_____

1. In the short story, Sue Phillips has brown eyes. What could her Genotype be?

2. The character Dave has blue eyes. What is his Genotype?

Most problems in Human Genetics are not as simple as the previous examples. Although only two genes determine whether the eyes will be brown or blue, other genes can modify the shade of the color and result in green and hazel eyes.

The story mentions that Sergeant Miles has male pattern baldness. This condition involves a gradual loss of hair on top of the head. It is caused by a sex-influenced gene. The gene's dominance is influenced by the sex of the bearer. The gene for pattern baldness is a dominant gene in males and a recessive gene in females.

Let P stand for the gene for pattern baldness.
Let n stand for the gene for not having pattern baldness.

Complete the following Table:

Genotype	Phenotype	
	In Males	In Females
pp	_____	Bald
Pn	_____	Not Bald
nn	Not Bald _____	

b. Food and Nutrition

This topic has been developed from the following words: hungry, food, breakfast, lunch, and dinner.

Food is the source of energy for our cells. The energy value of a food is measured in the amount of heat it will produce when burned in oxygen. The energy is measured in calories. (One calorie is the amount of heat required to raise the temperature of one gram of water one degree centigrade). Our digestive system breaks down food into a form that can be used by the cells. Food is used to build and maintain all our body systems. The amount of food needed each day depends on our body size and activities.

A good diet provides the right number of calories and the right types of food. The types of food that we need come from four main groups. These are the milk group, the meat group, the fruit and vegetable group, and the grain group. The milk group includes dairy products such as cheese, yogurt, and milk. The meat group includes meat, fish and eggs. The grain group includes breads and cereals.

Nutrition is the science that determines the food needs of people and other organisms. Humans need proteins, carbohydrates, fats, minerals, vitamins, and water. Proteins are mainly tissue builders. The amino acids that they provide are used to make all the different body proteins. Good sources of proteins are fish, meat, poultry, eggs, milk, and cheese. Carbohydrates provide the body with most of its energy. Sources of carbohydrates include sugar, bread, cereals, potatoes, rice, and pasta. Fats supply the body with energy. They are found in butter, lard, margarine, nuts, and oils. Minerals are needed by the body. Two important minerals are calcium and iron. Calcium is found in milk products and is important for proper development of bones and teeth. Iron is needed by red blood cells and is found in liver, meat, eggs, and green leafy vegetables. Vitamins are chemicals that are needed in small amounts by the body. Some important vitamins are: A, C, D, and K. Vitamin A is found in carrots and yellow vegetables and is essential for good vision. Vitamin C is found in citrus fruits and is important in tissue maintenance. Vitamin D is found in liver and eggs and promotes strong bones and teeth. Vitamin K is found in meat and green leafy vegetables and is essential to blood clotting.

Water makes up over half of our body weight. Its body uses include the break down of foods and the transporting of waste products.

Find words in the story that name foods. List them appropriately on the chart provided.

Four Food Groups

Milk Group

_____

_____

_____

_____

_____

_____

Meat Group

_____

_____

_____

_____

_____

_____

Fruit & Vegetable Group

_____

_____

_____

_____

_____

Grain Group

_____

_____

_____

_____

_____

Divide the class into the four food groups. Require each group to provide a nutritious snack for the class and to make an oral presentation discussing the importance of that snack.

One may further develop the topic of food and nutrition into a discussion of the digestive system and a discussion of diseases caused by improper diet.

c. Plants

This topic has been developed from the following words: weeping willow, tree, woods, grass, and flowers.

Plants are organisms that contain chlorophyll and make their own food in the presence of sunlight. They usually have roots that anchor them to the ground.

The two main types of plants are tracheophytes and bryophytes. Tracheophytes have special cells that move food, minerals, and water from one part of a plant to another. These plants have roots, stems, and leaves, and are capable of storing water. These plants include trees, cacti, and flowering plants. Bryophytes are usually small and have no real root systems, leaves, or stems. They cannot store or move water. Bryophytes live in moist regions. Mosses are a common type of bryophyte.

Most Plants Contain the Following Main Parts:
1. Roots- They anchor the plant and take in minerals from the soil.

2. Stems- They carry substances from the roots to the top of the plant.

3. Leaves- They contain chlorophyll. They make the food for the plant.

4. Seeds- These are the undeveloped offspring of the plant.

5. Fruit- This part of the plant contains the seeds.

6. Flowers- These contain the reproductive organs of the plant.

Plants are very useful to us. They provide us with food and many household products.

1. Make a list of the words in the story that name food plants (Hint: corn).

2. Make a list of the words in the story that name products from plants (Hint: paper is made from trees).

3. Using soil, Styrofoam cups, and seeds, have each student plant a seed and watch it grow.

One may go into a more detailed discussion of plants and discuss plant growth and reproduction.

Chapter 9

The short story, "Mail Mystery," contains science terms. Below is a list of the science terms and their definitions. Teachers may use these terms for classroom discussion topics.

Air- This is a mixture of gases. It contains about twenty percent oxygen, an element essential to life.

Chemistry- This is an area of science that deals with the structure, composition, and properties of substances. It also deals with reactions of substances.

Chloroform - This is a colorless, volatile liquid used as an anesthetic ($CHCl_3$).

Forensic Science - This is the application of science to a criminal investigation in order to provide evidence to solve the crime. Forensic scientists may testify as expert witnesses in criminal trials (ex. A forensic pathologist may perform an autopsy on a victim to determine the cause of sudden or unexpected death).

Ice - This is the solid form of water.

Moon - This is a celestial body that revolves around the earth. It may be a satellite that revolves around any planet.

Prey- This is one that is being hunted. The hunter is called the "predator."

Sound - This is that which can be heard. It is produced by an object vibrating, moving back and forth. The vibrating motion can be caused by hitting, blowing, and plucking. Sound moves from one particle to another by wave motion called "sound waves."

Water - This is a liquid consisting of two atoms of hydrogen and one atom of oxygen (H_2O). It is the universal solvent.

Work - This is equal to force times distance. It is the moving of a force through a distance.

Chapter 10

Application of the Problem-Solving Model

Report of Investigation

1. PROBLEM- A woman has been murdered and Sue Phillips is missing.

2. AVAILABLE INFORMATION- Sue Phillips discovered a dead body while delivering mail. Sue and James Brown reported the incident to the cops. James Brown, the Rome postal clerk, was one of the last people to see Sue before she disappeared. Other information: victim's body; victim's apartment; victim's name: Leslie Jones; victim's age: thirty years old; victim's place of employment: secretary for the law firm Briggs and Grows; victim's time of death: 11:00 a.m.

3. OTHER NEEDED DATA- Motive for crimes, witnesses, and suspects.

4. PROCEDURE TO OBTAIN NEEDED DATA- Cops must do a thorough investigation. (Check Leslie's apartment, her friends, her place of employment, etc., go on Sue's mail route and ask people if they saw her, and interview James Brown.)

Report of Investigation Continued

5. PROCEDURE TO OBTAIN NEEDED DATA- Cops interviewed James Brown, Cops interviewed Leslie's employers, Cops

searched Leslie's apartment, and Cops got valuable information from Leslie's diary.

6. RECORD THE DATA- James Brown dropped Sue off at Chestnut Street. Leslie's employers said that she had been employed just under three years and that she was quiet and kept to herself. They said that Leslie had a boy friend named Joe and that she left work for a morning appointment on the day of the murder. A diary with valuable data (could be listed here in number 6 as well as in number 5) was found in Leslie's apartment.

7. ORGANIZE THE DATA-MOTIVES: Silence Leslie's drug knowledge and silence Sue (a possible witness to murder).

Leslie's Diary Data

Name	Place	Time	Event
Joe Larson	Big Apple in Rome	Dinner Time May 15, 1970	Dinner Date Office Party
Joe Larson	Joe's Home in the Woods	Day June 20, 1970	Leslie told Joe that she suspected that he and his friends were running a drug ring.
Joe Larson	Leslie's Home	Evening July 8, 1970	Joe called & made an appointment to meet Leslie at her apartment on the morning of July 9.

Sue Phillips discovers Leslie's body and Sue disappears on July 9. James Brown—possibly last person to see Sue. He dropped her off at Chestnut Street.

8. ANALYZE THE DATA- Closely study all the data.

9. GENERALIZE FROM THE DATA- Joe Larson had been dating Leslie. He and his friends were most likely involved with drugs. Leslie was murdered the morning of July 9, 1970. Joe and/or his friends were responsible for Leslie's death. The disappearance of Sue Phillips is related to this crime. Sue may have been a witness to the crime.

10. DECISION MAKING- Locate and visit Joe Larson's house. Capture him and his friends. Save Sue Phillips.

Application of the Science Process Skills

Science Process Skill	Level of Learning
Observing	Knowledge

Behavioral Objectives

1. Leslie Jones, Sue Phillips, James Brown, Joe Larson, Dave, Sergeant Miles, Smitty, Dan Phillips, Angela Phillips, and Mr. Lawrence.

2. Leslie Jones- a murdered secretary, described as young and quiet.

   Sue Phillips- a pretty college student with brown eyes and brown hair. She has a summer job as a substitute mail carrier.

   Joe Larson- He is a young man involved in drugs. He knew Leslie.

   Dave- a good-looking man about thirty years old. He has black wavy hair and dark blue eyes. He is involved in drugs.

   Sergeant Miles- A highly respected cop in Rome who has solved many crimes. He is a rotund man with male pattern baldness.

   Smitty- an energetic cop who is like a right hand to Sergeant Miles.

Dan Phillips- Sue's father. He is an inspector at Griffis Air Force Base in Rome, New York.

Angela Phillips- She is Dan's wife and Sue's mother. She is the perfect mother and an excellent cook.

Mr. Lawrence- He is the postmaster of the Rome Post Office. He is a small-framed man with blue eyes and grey hair. He is a serious person.

3. The story takes place in Rome, New York.

4. The story takes place in July of 1970.

5. Sue Phillips lives in Clinton, near Hamilton College.

Science Process Skill	Level of Learning
Classifying	Knowledge

Behavioral Objectives

1. Phillips' Family- Dan, Angela, and Sue

2. Post Office Workers- Sue Phillips, Mr. Lawrence, Tom Johnson, James Brown, Jackson, and Peterson

3. Cops- Sergeant Miles and Smitty

4. Lawyers- Johnathan Briggs and Nathan Grows

Science Process Skill	Level of Learning
Interpreting Data	Comprehension

Behavioral Objectives

1. This means to deliver mail on your own with no assistance.

2. This means that in their line of work they can't take any risks.

3. This means that I finally met someone more intelligent than I am.

Science Process Skill	Level of Learning
Measuring	Comprehension

Behavioral Objectives

1. Sue Phillips is about twenty years old because she is a junior in college.

2. Most of the story takes place in three days. (Day 1- Sue delivers mail with Tom Johnson. Day 2- Sue discovers a body & Sue disappears. Day 3- Sue is rescued.)

Science Process Skill   Level of Learning
Using Numbers   Application

Behavioral Objectives

1. 18 houses received mail.

2. 35 houses received mail.

Science Process Skill   Level of Learning
Inferring   Analysis

Behavioral Objectives

1. Sue had a fear of dogs and was nervous in their presence.

2. Mr. Lawrence felt guilty about Sue's disappearance. He was weary because he had spent much of the previous night worrying about Sue.

3. Sergeant Miles is a brave, courageous, and intelligent cop.

Science Process Skill   Level of Learning
Predicting   Synthesis

Behavioral Objectives

1. Many answers exist.

2. Many answers exist.

Science Process Skill   Level of Learning
Interpreting Data   Evaluation

Behavioral Objectives

1. Dan Phillips and James Brown are similar in that they both appear to be caring and concerned individuals. They also differ. Dan is sincerely a good person on the inside as well as his outward appearance. James Brown appears to be good, but one later finds out that he is a criminal and involved with drugs.

2. They want to silence Sue to protect themselves. In the drug business they can't take any chances. Sue is a threat to them.

3. Sue shouldn't be silenced. She didn't witness the crime and therefore isn't a threat to the criminals. Also, murder is against the law.

Science Activities

Topic a.: Human Genetics

Punnett Square

	B	b
B	BB	Bb
b	bB	bb

Genotype of Offspring	Phenotype of Offspring
BB	Brown Eyes
Bb	Brown Eyes
bB	Brown Eyes
bb	Blue Eyes

Punnett Square

	B	B
b	bB	bB
b	bB	bB

Genotype of Offspring	Phenotype of Offspring
bB	Brown Eyes
bB	Brown Eyes
bB	Brown Eyes
bB	Brown Eyes

1. BB or Bb
2. bb

Genotype	Phenotype	
	In Males	In Females
pp	Bald	Bald
Pn	Bald	Not Bald
nn	Not Bald	Not Bald

Topic b.: Food and Nutrition

Four Food Groups

Milk Group
Drink (Milk)
Butter

Meat Group
Ham
Chicken
Hot Dogs
Hamburger
Meatballs

Fruit & Vegetable Group
Potatoes
Corn
Strawberry
Apple
Salads

Grain Group
Toast
Rolls
Shortcake
Spaghetti

Topic c.: Plants

1. Corn, Potatoes, Strawberry, Apple

2. Paper, Chair, Books, Table, Desk, House, Door, Floor, Couch, Garage, Shingles, Stairs, Newspapers, Porch (these products are made from trees).

References

Barry, Dana M. and Hideyuki Kanematsu. "International Program to Promote Creative Thinking in Chemistry and Science," *The Chemist*, 10 (June 2006).

Barry, Dana M. and Hideyuki Kanematsu (representing M.S. & E. Department Faculty at SNCT). *Science Fair Fun in Japan*. Gendai Tosho, Japan (2005).

Barry, Dana M. and James F. Barry. "Growth Potential." *Science Scope* (Science Sampler), 36 (April 2004).

Barry, Dana M. and James F. Barry. "In-Disposable Diapers." *The Science Teacher* (Idea Bank), 61 (February 2004).

Barry, Dana M., Hideyuki Kanematsu, Tatsumasa Kobayashi, and Hiroshi Shimofuruya. "Using the Senses to Turn Students onto Chemistry: A Comparison between the United States and Japan. *The Chemist*, 13 (Summer 2003).

Barry, Dana M., Hideyuki Kanematsu, Tatsumasa Kobayashi, and Hiroshi Shimofuruya. "Multi-Sensory Science," *The Science Teacher* (Idea Bank), 66 (May 2003).

Barry, Dana M. *Science Fair Projects: Helping Your Child Create A Super Science Fair Project.* Teacher Created Materials. California (2000).

Learning Standards for Mathematics, Science, and Technology. New York (March 1996 & Forward).

Miller, Kenneth R. and Joseph Levine. *Biology* (5th edition). Prentice-Hall: New Jersey (2000).

The Ontario Curriculum: Science and Technology, (Grades 1–8), Ministry of Education (1998).

About the Authors

Dana M. Barry (Ph.D., C.P.C.) is the President of Ansted University's Scientific Board and Senior Technical Writer/Editor at Clarkson University's Center for Advanced Materials Processing (CAMP). She is a certified professional chemist and has permanent teacher certification in chemistry and the general sciences grades 7–12 in New York State. Dana is a member of the National Science Teachers Association, the American Institute of Chemists and its Editorial Review Board, and of the Northern New York Section of the American Chemical Society, where she serves as an officer. She organized three World First Space Missions and served as a Visiting Professor in Malaysia (2001), Japan (2002), England (2003), Malaysia (2004), and Japan (2005). She has numerous honors to her name and over one hundred professional publications, including six books. Dana received APEX Awards for Publication Excellence eleven years in a row (1996–2006) from Communications Concepts in Springfield, VA. Her Chemical Sensation Project and World First MarsLink Space Mission Program received National Awards from the American Chemical Society (August 2004). In addition, Dana's biographical profile is listed in the Outstanding Gale Reference *Something About the Author* (Volume 139, June 2003) and has been selected for inclusion in *Marquis Who's Who in American Education* (7th Edition, 2006–2007) , *Marquis Who's Who of American Women* (25th Edition, 2006–2007), and *Marquis Who's Who in Science and Engineering* (9th Edition, 2006–2007).

Hideyuki Kanematsu (Ph.D. MIMF) is an Associate Professor for Suzuka National College of Technology in Japan and a researcher for

Heat-Surface Treatment Engineering. He is a certified professional member of the Institute for Metal Finishing in the United Kingdom (MIMF) and also a member of many professional societies in the USA and Japan, such as American Electroplaters and the Surface Finishing Society (AESF), Japan Institute of Metals (JIM) and The Iron and Steel Institute of Japan (ISIJ). Besides his engineering research, he has been interested in global collaborations for engineering education. In particular his collaboration with Dr. Dana Barry of Clarkson University, USA, has brought him some great honors. He received an Outstanding Achievement Award from the Northern New York Section of the American Chemical Society (2002) and a Presidential Award from the Association of National Colleges of Technology in Japan (2003). Dr. Kanematsu's biographical profile is listed in *Marquis Who's Who in Science and Engineering* (5th Edition, 1999) and *Marquis Who's Who in the World* (18th Edition, 2000). He has also been selected for inclusion in *Marquis Who's Who in Science and Engineering* (9th Edition, 2006–2007) and *Marquis Who's Who in Asia* (2007).

Other Books by the Authors:

Science Fair Fun in Japan

Science Fair Projects

Easy Chemistry

Simple Chemistry

 LIVE

listen|imagine|view|experience

AUDIO BOOK DOWNLOAD INCLUDED WITH THIS BOOK!

In your hands you hold a complete digital entertainment package. Besides purchasing the paper version of this book, this book includes a free download of the audio version of this book. Simply use the code listed below when visiting our website. Once downloaded to your computer, you can listen to the book through your computer's speakers, burn it to an audio CD or save the file to your portable music device (such as Apple's popular iPod) and listen on the go!

How to get your free audio book digital download:

1. Visit www.tatepublishing.com and click on the e|LIVE logo on the home page.
2. Enter the following coupon code:
   567d-26af-6336-1023-4b32-9e59-fb1e-6768
3. Download the audio book from your e|LIVE digital locker and begin enjoying your new digital entertainment package today!